This delightful book gives us not only a touching snapshot in time but a moving look at a family and an art during Nashville's most exciting years. This is a book to treasure.

—RANGER DOUG,
Riders in the Sky

Les Leverett's photographs of a wonderful era, in tandem with Libby's recollections, give us a deeper insight not just to the times but also to these two special people, the love they have for life and for all who knew them.

—EDDIE STUBBS,
WSM *Grand Ole Opry* Announcer

Wow, what a thrill it must have been to grow up with Grand Ole Opry photographer Les Leverett and see all the things that Libby saw. How cool is that!

—RICKY SKAGGS

SATURDAY NIGHTS WITH DADDY

AT THE OPRY

SATURDAY NIGHTS WITH DADDY

AT THE OPRY

Libby Leverett-Crew

Rutledge Hill Press®
Nashville, Tennessee

A Division of Thomas Nelson, Inc.
www.ThomasNelson.com

Published by Rutledge Hill Press, a Division of Thomas Nelson, Inc., P.O. Box 141000,
Nashville, Tennessee, 37214.

Library of Congress Cataloging-in-Publication Data

Leverett Crew, Libby, 1960-
   Saturday nights with Daddy at the Opry / by Libby Leverett Crew.
      p. cm.
   Includes index.
   ISBN 1-4016-0114-6 (hardcover)
   1. Country musicians. 2. Leverett, Les. 3. Grand ole opry (Radio program)
   4. Leverett Crew, Libby, 1960- I. Title.
   ML394.L48 2003
   781.642'09768'55—dc22

                                                              2003015004

Printed in the United States of America

03 04 05 06 07 — 5 4 3 2 1

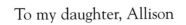

To my daughter, Allison

TABLE OF CONTENTS

FOREWORD

It just seems like yesterday that Libby was accompanying her father, Les, as he was photographing the country music stars that appeared on the *Opry*. This book was like entering into another time, a very special time. In those days, we had no idea how insightful and perceptive she was. We do now!

She paints such vivid pictures with her words that the reader feels he or she is right there visiting with these country music celebrities. This should not amaze us, since her father, as the official *Opry* photographer, had a keen eye for detail. He taught her well.

She allows us to see, through a child's eyes, the country music stars as they were off the stage. Libby's impressions, honest yet innocent, are so revealing and engaging that it is hard to put this book down. From the easy laughter and openness of Minnie Pearl, a.k.a. Sarah Cannon, to the biting wit of Grandpa Jones to the uninhibited frankness of Loretta Lynn, we see glimpses of the real people beyond the glitter of their stardom.

Of course, what moved us the most were Libby's recollections of our parents, which reminded us of their playful love and the delight that they had for each other. It brought tears to our eyes and joy to our hearts.

So, for those of you who are country music fans, this book provides a new perspective, and it is a welcome addition to your country music library. For those of you who are new to country music, this is a memorable introduction.

Either way, enjoy the read!

TOM AND JOHN RITTER

PREFACE

I depended a lot upon my memory to write this book and tried to keep everything as historically accurate as possible. It has been a fun project to recall memories and go through old photographs and negatives with my dad. My whole family told stories, laughed, and cried together for hours and days on end.

The Ryman Auditorium was once called the "The Mother Church." Even with gum stuck on the underside of the pews, the stench of stale cigarette smoke and buttery popcorn, and the loud, loud music, there was something reverential about that building. Its walls hold the memories of many songs and the happy spirits of the well-entertained. It also holds some of my fondest memories of being with my family and friends during a good part of my childhood.

I have the blessing of having had two supportive parents in my life. As my mother will attest from her own experience with her dad, there is just something special about the father-daughter bond. Being able to go to work with my dad, to actually see what he did in order to keep us clothed, sheltered, and fed gave me a great appreciation for his sacrifice and gave me a strong sense of responsibility.

I hope that this account touches you, helps you recall some of your own memories, and gives you hope. And, if there are children in your life, make sure you stay involved with them. Let them go to work with you. Give them an idea of how much you love them. If there is not a child in your life, borrow one. I guarantee you will not only brighten your own life but will give someone else a pack of memories to keep forever and carry into the future. And always, keep music in your life.

AUTHOR'S NOTE:

If someone's story is told, how could they completely be gone from us? Maybe this is why I write. Today, when I received the sad news that Johnny Cash and John Ritter had both died within hours of each other, this book was already in the process of being typeset.

Johnny had been awfully ill and he missed his late wife June so very much. His death was a terrible loss to us all, but in my heart, I believe it was a gift for him. A part of me rejoices in his peace.

Johnny's death had been expected, but John's was a shock that left my mind unable to focus, and my heart heavy with sadness. I called to check on John's brother, and my dear friend, Tom. He wanted me to know that one of the last things that he and John had done together was to read this book (in preparation to write the foreword). He reminded me that John especially liked the ending of the chapter on their family.

A comforting thought came to me, Endings are never what they seem.

It is my sincere hope that the stories included in this book bring honor to both the Cash and the Ritter families and that having their stories told will help keep their memories alive.

LIBBY LEVERETT-CREW
Nashville, September 12, 2003

ACKNOWLEDGMENTS

Of course, I would first like to thank my father, Les Leverett, who made this book possible. If I had not had so many adventures with you, I would not have these memories to share. Thanks for digging for hours through negatives and prints for this book. It would not be the same without the photos. Thank you for reading to me when I was little and for always keeping me in books. Thanks to my mother, Dot Vandiver Leverett, for laughing with me at greeting card stands, keeping me in art supplies, sharing her love of poetry, teaching me to color, cook, and sew, and encouraging me to try my wings. She is the most unselfish, giving person I have ever known. Thank you to my brother, Gary Leverett, who shares my history and makes me laugh. He introduced me to some great music in my youth and made sure I had the best concert tickets. To the memory of my late brother, John, whose passing reminded me to write this book. Thank you to Bryan Curtis who believed in this project and went to bat for it in its infancy. I respect your honesty. Thank you, Lisa Broussard, for doing your magic with the cover. Thank you Doug, Marty, Dolly, Ricky, and Eddie for your support. My special thanks to John Reiman for your professional help, advice, and encouragement. Thank you to Tom, Dana, and Mackenzie Cunningham, who gave me time to write and a safe, fun place for Allison to be while I did so. Thanks to Jan Blaustone. You have now witnessed the realization of two of my most fantastic dreams. Thanks for being there. Thank you to Mary Hall Anderson, my first and sixth grade teacher, who always, always believed in me. I still have *If*, by Rudyard Kipling, in the back of my mind on most days. Thank you, Rineke van Beek, my "Dutch sister." You remind me that music is truly universal.

Thanks to Lou Dozier for always giving me good books. Thanks to Tom and Mary Nell Breeden who gave me their orchard in which to dream and their condo in the mountains in which to write. Thank you Alisa, Peggy, Helen, Lynne, Julie, Alice, Joe, Jerry & Laurel, Faith, Shug, Jennifer & Dave, Janice, Myra, Sandra, Dave A., Cheri, Bill & Connie, Anna, and Susan for your friendship and encouragement along the way. To the memory of Shannon and of Vic Willis, two of my favorite funny people whose laughter is forever with me. To my aunt, Cynthia Vandiver Dye, the original party animal, for teaching me to dance and for making all the family gatherings festive. Thank you, Laura, for giving me the most precious gift I have ever received. To Larry, my soul mate, thanks for doing all the domestic stuff while I wrote this book. You were there when this project first came to me and when all the other dreams were born. You're up next. To Allison, my own personal angel disguised as my daughter, let this book be an example that you should always believe in your dreams. Oh, and thank you for my second childhood. It sure is fun. And finally, thank you to all of the music makers of the world. You bring us all together.

INTRODUCTION

How odd to find myself in the backseat of a large, dark car with two Secret Service agents sitting up front. The rain pounded on the windshield as we three looked anxiously toward the sky for a small jet. The area around the small, private airport was blocked off for security. We were the only humans in sight. As I double-checked my cameras and changed lenses, the agents carried on a normal conversation about their weekend, while occasionally talking into small microphones hidden in their shirtsleeves. They were confirming landing time, along with ground travel instructions, and I heard one mention, "Yes, she's with us."

Fascinated, I finally asked just how much they learned from the social security number I had given them for security clearance before I could shoot this job. They seemed to know everything. They knew that I did not go by my legal name. They knew my husband's full name, that he was from Virginia, that he had a perfect driving record, and that together we owned our house. I had never been convicted of a felony. I was a second-generation photographer. (They knew this because my father had been through security clearance when he had photographed, over the years, former presidents John F. Kennedy, Lyndon B. Johnson, Richard Nixon, Gerald Ford, Jimmy Carter, Ronald Reagan, and George H. W. Bush.) They knew my father and I both worked mainly in the music industry and that sometimes we worked together. Amazing! I felt naked before these guys.

The rain subsided just in time for the jet to land directly in front of us. The agents jumped out of the car, totally alert and cautious. I was ready

President Jimmy Carter and First Lady Rosalynn arriving in Nashville at a private airport. PHOTOGRAPH BY LIBBY LEVERETT-CREW.

to work, with my camera around my neck and my lens cap in my pocket. One of the agents opened the door on the jet. Out stepped another agent, then former President Jimmy Carter and his wife, Rosalynn. She spotted me immediately and said, "Well, hi there! How are you today?" President Carter nodded to me and in his great Georgia accent asked, "How awe yah?" I felt like their long lost next-door neighbor. Of course, I was the only nonofficial there, so I guess they felt obliged to speak and be kind. I photographed them in front of the jet, and they thanked me over and over. Jimmy said, "See yah latah!" They got in the backseat of a limousine, which had appeared while I was working, and rode off to give a speech at the Opryland Hotel.

I stood there, completely alone and in total disbelief. I had just photographed a former president of the United States of America. We had exchanged pleasantries. All of a sudden, I realized that I was leading a most interesting life.

This not-so-typical existence all began back when I could not hold my own bottle, when I toddled among the rhinestones and sharply-pointed cowboy boots backstage at the Ryman Auditorium while Daddy worked photographing the *Grand Ole Opry* radio show—a live radio

Libby's mother, Dot, with Liberace onstage at Fan Fair in 1963. PHOTOGRAPH BY LES LEVERETT.

show. The *Opry* began in 1925, being broadcast from the National Life and Accident Insurance Company building on WSM-AM radio 650. Among other venues, the Ryman Auditorium—the Mother Church—housed the *Grand Ole Opry* from 1943 until 1974, when it was moved to the current Opry House.

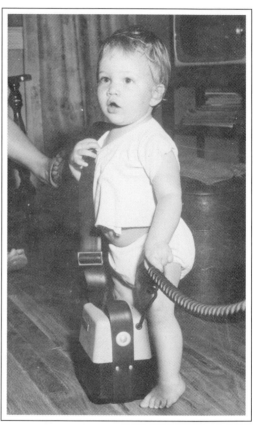

Going to work with my photographer daddy in Nashville's music industry and rubbing elbows with some of the most famous people in the world felt as natural to me as children in Iowa probably feel going into the fields to plant corn with their father. I was enthralled just to be with him. It did not matter what he was doing or where we were. I was with my daddy and that was all that mattered. I was so conditioned to respect and admire the good in all people and learn the lessons they had to teach me that it never really sank in that some of my life's experiences were beyond the ordinary.

Libby Leverett-Crew in 1961 at age one, carrying her daddy's camera equipment. PHOTOGRAPH BY LES LEVERETT.

There was no particular moment in which I realized that my heart was in the same place as my daddy's, and I was meant to view life as he did—through a lens. I was living a lifetime apprenticeship.

This apprenticeship took me behind the scenes and on the stages of

some very exciting events. Through my daddy, I have been in the company of and have photographed famous actors and actresses, presidents, poets, artists, rock 'n' roll stars, ballet dancers, opera singers, musicians, astronauts, Muppets, professional football players, comedians, and everyday people who change our world in ways no one knows about.

Les Leverett and Libby Leverett-Crew at the Opryland Hotel in 1988, on an evening when they were both photographing the same job. FROM THE COLLECTION OF LES LEVERETT.

More than the lights and excitement of growing up in this industry, I have been given a gift much greater: a daddy who spent time with me and seemed to have known what I was going to need to take with me on my own journey through life. And I'm not talking about a camera bag.

SANDBOX DREAMS

My sandbox was a gift from Daddy. It was painted bright red enamel and sat beneath the old hackberry trees in our side yard.

I remember feeling at peace with my young world on those sunny, carefree days in my sandbox. My mind would open up to all kinds of ideas and questions, and from there the wonders of childhood were magnified tenfold. It was a spiritual experience.

On cool days, the windows of our house would be open, and I could hear the radio playing from inside. My mother loved Jim Reeves' smooth voice, and I could hear her singing along with him as she did the dishes. It made me feel safe and content. From time to time, I would join in, and all the birds in those hackberry trees would scatter to the winds.

Many early Saturday mornings, Daddy would set up a card table on our back porch. He would bring out newspapers, a sticky bottle of turpentine, a collection of sticks about the size of soda straws, a roll of cotton, his Marshall Oil Paints, and a large, mounted black and white portrait of some *Opry* member that he had taken the week before. This would draw me out of my sandbox and to his side where I would watch him prepare this photograph for handcoloring.

He would talk to me as he worked and explained each step of the process, squeezing out little dabs of different hues and giving me the correct name for each color as he did so. (Magenta, cyan, vermilion, burnt umber, etc.) He would place a stick on the tip of his tongue to dampen it and would then roll it in a little tuft of cotton he held between his fingers. For smaller areas, he would do the same with toothpicks.

When it became too cold or too windy for Daddy to hand color photographs on the back porch, he would move his work inside, near a window. The strong smell of oil paint and turpentine was almost over-whelming, but in an odd way, I liked it. As I got older, he would pre-pare an extra photograph for me to practice on, and I would sit by his side, copying his every move.

One March night, when I was six years old, my daddy, who colored those photos in an old, paint-stained, ragged shirt, wearing flip-flops on his feet, became a Grammy award-winning photographer.

The night of the awards, I thought my parents had turned into roy-alty. Daddy was handsome in his black tux and cummerbund, and Mom was beautiful beyond words in her gold dress and matching shoes. I had been shipped off to a sitter for the evening, not really knowing how important this night was going to be.

Les Leverett giving his acceptance speech at the Grammy Awards in 1967. FROM THE COLLECTION OF LES LEVERETT.

I remember being awakened by Mom and Dad when they came in all excited early the next morning. Something about a Grammy was mentioned, and Daddy showed me a brass gramophone mounted on wood with a little brass plaque with his name on it. I thought it was cute. I went back to sleep.

Les Leverett and his Grammy in 1967. PHOTOGRAPH BY DOT LEVERETT.

I understood more the following day when I returned to my first-grade class and everyone was talking about how Libby's daddy had his picture in the newspaper that morning. Miss Hall, our teacher, gave us the morning off to celebrate by making a congratulatory book for Daddy. She explained to the class how my father had won an award for Best Album Cover of the Year for *Confessions of a Broken Man*, a Porter Wagoner album.

I presented the book of letters and crayon drawings from my first-grade class, still damp with paste, to Daddy that evening. It brought tears to his eyes.

Life in the Leverett household quickly went back to normal. My Grammy-winning daddy still had to go to work. We kids still had to go to school, and Mom still had to do the dishes and laundry. All of this living continued around the Grammy, which held a place of prominence on a dusty shelf in our living room.

On weekdays, when Daddy would leave for work, he would remind me to spend time outside and enjoy all that I saw and did. I took his advice. I would explore the creek in the back of our yard and catch tadpoles and crawdads. I would fly to other places and perform in circus acts on the tire swing he and my brothers had hung in a large tree for me. I would climb to my favorite branch on my favorite climbing tree, imagining I was on my way up Mt. Everest.

Even with all those other adventures, I always ended up in my sandbox.

Sometimes, I would dig with sticks down below the sand into the damp mud below, breaking those twigs by the dozen in my quest to see China. Someone once told me to be careful; I might miss China and see the Devil instead. I was too smart for that though. I knew I was going to China and expected to pop up in some Chinaman's colorful garden.

Through the planning and construction of that sandbox, Daddy was probably very well aware that he was giving my creative mind a place to grow and expand. This was one of the greatest gifts that I have ever

Libby and Oscar T. exploring the creek behind their home in 1963. PHOTOGRAPH BY LES LEVERETT.

received. He gave me the ocean in my backyard, right there in Tennessee. He knew that this was important.

He had always been a dreamer. A dreamer without a sandbox.

Daddy grew up in a tiny town in southern Alabama. He didn't have a sandbox, but he didn't need one. Sand occurs naturally in that area of the country. It is tracked into every house south of Birmingham and has been upsetting clean and tidy homemakers for generations. It is a pale tan, almost white shade, and if mixed with the orange clay-like soil of southern Alabama, it could hold more than sandboxes together.

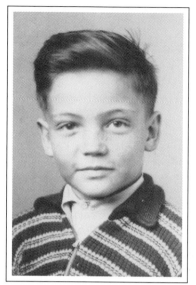

Les Leverett as a young schoolboy in Alabama. PHOTOGRAPHER UNKNOWN.

When Daddy was a young boy, he was playing in that sand on the side of a street where few cars traveled back in the early thirties. A cow had just been by and left behind a large pile of "evidence." Dad covered the still warm manure with a coating of sand, ran straight to his best friend Hector's house, and asked if he could come play. His mom said Hector was just finishing dinner and would be right out. Dad yelled through the screen door to him that if Hector hurried, he would let him be the first one to jump into the sand pile he had just made. Hector came out the door, chocolate cake in hand, ran full speed ahead, and before that screen door could smack its frame, he jumped and splashed into that "sandpile." It was an explosion of sand, fresh manure, and Devil's food cake. Dad says that he doesn't think Hector's mom ever got over it.

Those early days in Alabama were a challenge for Daddy's family, but from a child's perspective, they were probably as carefree as my summer days in that sandbox. I'm sure the humor helped keep them alive. There was not much to eat. People would pay his evangelist father for preaching with fresh-grown vegetables, fruits, and meats. Someone gave them an old cow so that the family would have a good supply of milk and butter. And thank God for peanuts. Peanuts were very plentiful in Alabama and kept many a family from starvation.

When I was a child, we would take the long trip to southern Alabama to see Daddy's mother, my Mammaw. We would usually arrive in Atmore late at night. We would visit by the light of the bare bulb that hung from the middle of her living room ceiling. Wallpaper with designs of large flowers covered some of the walls and newspaper covered others. The lace curtains would blow in and out of the window, and the hum of the fan was in fierce competition with the sound of the train whose tracks lay on the other side of the street.

Les's mother, Hassie Mae Leverett, and Libby in Alabama in 1961. PHOTOGRAPH BY LES LEVERETT.

If we were in Atmore on a Saturday evening, the radio would be tuned to our country music station back home in Nashville. Dad would comment on who was on the *Grand Ole Opry* program that particular night, and I could tell that he missed it. He loved his work as *Opry* photographer. He had listened to the *Opry* on that same old, popping, crackling radio when he was a boy. Now, he lived in Nashville and the *Opry* was a large part of his life. It also became a large part of my life.

During our visits to Mammaw's, I would hang out with Daddy in the yard. We would walk slowly around every inch of that small enclosure.

Les's childhood home on Wilson Avenue in Atmore, Alabama. PHOTOGRAPH BY LES LEVERETT.

Together, we would run our fingers over the smooth, velvety seedpods of the wisteria bush. We would inhale the fragrance from the lilac and marvel at the way the pecan trees had grown. The texture of the bark on the pecan trees would interest us, then an anthill would draw us in and we would watch the busy activity with awe. Daddy would point out some tiny ant carrying a load that would equal a human carrying a car.

I loved being with Daddy and his memories in that yard. He loved the details of life. He and I have always shared the joy of watching bugs at work, flowers in bloom, and birds in flight. I learned from him that fine points were important, that details were essential to his and eventually my chosen field of photography. The influences of such things as watching ants and smelling flowers have affected my work more than anything else that I can name besides having literally grown up in front of a camera.

Four-year-old Libby in her father's studio in Nashville in 1964.
PHOTOGRAPH BY LES LEVERETT.

On many occasions, Daddy would sneak up on me to capture what I was doing on film. At a very early age, I began to be able to sense when he and that camera were near, but I continued like I didn't until I heard the shutter click, and then I'd throw him a knowing glance. He usually caught that on film, too. Sometimes, he would need a model for an ad, and I worked cheap. For an hour's work, I charged one treat from the ice cream man.

A couple of times a year, Mom and I would go meet Daddy at his studio in downtown Nashville to have my formal portrait done. My brothers avoided this as often as they could. He would talk me through several different poses and would change backdrops a few times throughout the session. All the pretty colored and designed backdrops looked like giant rolls of Christmas paper hanging from the tall ceiling of that studio. I watched in amazement as he would crank the huge sheets of paper back to the ceiling and then crank another one down. As he set his camera up and changed film, I would half listen to his and Mom's conversation and would take in all of the boom lights, colored gels over hot bulbs, and the way that my daddy could do three or four things at once while he was working.

At Christmas time, my brothers, sulking as usual, and I would dress in our best and be Dad's subjects for the annual family greeting card. This

Gary and John . . . and Libby posing for the annual Christmas card in 1960. PHOTOGRAPH BY LES LEVERETT.

Grandpa Jones in the studio in Nashville in 1965. PHOTOGRAPH BY LES LEVERETT.

was always a great production with my mother acting as set designer and prop manager.

I was not aware that many *Opry* stars sat on that same stool to have their portraits taken by my daddy. Grandpa Jones, Patsy Cline, Minnie Pearl, Bill Monroe, Roy Acuff, Tex Ritter, Loretta Lynn, and so many more. I'm sure that they felt the same comfort and ease in being there as I felt, with Daddy talking to them and cracking jokes. He had a way of bringing out someone's personality for the film.

Patsy Cline in the studio in Nashville in 1961. PHOTOGRAPH BY LES LEVERETT.

Marty Robbins in the studio in Nashville in 1961. PHOTOGRAPH BY LES LEVERETT.

I like to believe that this trait was inherited from his father, a small town Alabama preacher man, who never held a camera, yet whose goo d humor and love for others made those around him feel like kindred spirits.

Atmore, Alabama, was just about seventy miles north of the Gulf of Mexico, almost close enough to smell the salt breezes on windy days. Daddy's father had acquired an old Ford Model-A. One day, he decided to drive Dad down the long, sandy roads to Gulf Shores for his first sight of the ocean. Daddy says that his life completely changed after that experience. The vastness of that body of water, the way you could see for miles, and the way that the ocean met the sky in the distance set his mind into

Les and his mother, Hassie Mae Leverett, in Alabama. PHOTOGRAPHER UNKNOWN.

motion. The crashing waves and the sea creatures he had never seen before fascinated him. These things made him realize that there was so much more outside the sandy streets of his childhood. There was a whole, huge sandbox out there waiting to be discovered and explored. He could not wait to see more.

When Daddy was fourteen, not long after his first trip to the beach, his father went off to work and didn't come home. Dad went to look for him, and friends and neighbors joined in the search. He was found dead on the trail from a heart attack. He was only fifty-two years old.

Suddenly Daddy was fatherless with the weight of the world on his shoulders. From that point on, he was responsible for his mother and younger sister. Schooling took a back seat.

Daddy was offered work at Anderson's Store on the main drag in Atmore. He swept and straightened shelves and eventually moved up to selling shoes and work clothes to the local farmers.

Even though he had to grow up fast, Daddy found time to keep his dreams alive. He saved his pennies to go after work to the Saturday afternoon movie matinee. The westerns he saw there made him dream about life out west, beyond the Mississippi River, and they sparked his love for western art. He read continually, buying or borrowing every book he could get his hands on. Saturday nights, the *Opry* was always on the radio. He listened to the music, the announcers, and the advertisements. The dreams of travel to distant places that were born that day at the beach would not go away.

The next thing Daddy knew, our country was in a war and he was in the service, training in Colorado to be a medic. He was off, discovering the sands in other places. By then, he was very interested in photography and had a little box camera. He marveled at the Front Range of the Rocky Mountains that was always the background to his photos. They were northwest of the base, and he could see them from his window. He slept every night in their shadow, little dreaming that four decades later, he would have a daughter living in those mountains and climbing them with her own camera around her neck.

Les Leverett outside his barracks in Denver, Colorado, at Fitzsimmons General (Army) Hospital. PHOTOGRAPHER UNKNOWN.

While stationed onboard the SS *Haverford Victory* he spent a lot of his time photographing the interesting people he met and the places he visited. He developed his film in a tiny room on the ship and sent his adventures home to Alabama in the form of small black and white photographs.

The war had taken Daddy from his southern Alabama home, and after World War II, Les Leverett never went back. His goal was to see the world and everything in it.

The Front Range of the Rocky Mountains at Bear Lake outside of Estes Park, Colorado. Long's Peak is on the left with snow on the top. PHOTOGRAPH BY LES LEVERETT.

Thanks to the G.I. Bill, after the war, Dad attended the Texas College of Photographic Art in San Antonio, Texas. It was in San Antonio where his best friend at the "A Happy Home" boarding house (named so they'd be listed first in the yellow pages) set him up with a blind date. Dot Vandiver was her name, and she hated blind dates. In fact, this was her *only* blind date.

It was a good thing she went. Les Leverett turned out to be the love of her life. They went to hear Bob Wills on that first date. That was after a dinner where Mom was hit in the face by a tortilla when she leaned over as Dad's friend was passing one, flying-saucer style, through the air to another friend. Five months later, they were married. Ten months after that, they had my brother, John. They lived in San Antonio for about a year and then moved back to Nashville, my mom's hometown, where Daddy got into his photography career. Not long after, another brother, Gary, was born.

I was the "caboose" and not born until my brothers were nine and eleven. I call my situation, "the second litter." It was akin to being an only child, and not a bad arrangement, with the exception of when I started dating; then, it seemed that I had three fathers.

Dot and Les Leverett's wedding in San Antonio, Texas, in 1949. PHOTOGRAPHER UNKNOWN.

I was the only girl in our household besides Mom. Although my mother and I have always been close, I was always a daddy's girl. When I would get my bath at night and my skin would wrinkle up from being in the water too long, I would yell, "Come get me Mine Daddy, I'm getting older by the minute!" My nickname for Daddy has sometimes been "Mine Daddy."

Daddy and I explored the creek in our backyard and the coastline of the Gulf. We watched the night skies together. He took me to work with him at the Ryman where the *Opry* was broadcast. Through him, I met people from every walk of life.

The Leverett children together with Dot's sister, Cynthia, at what was then Madison Hospital (TCMC) in 1960. John is holding newborn Libby, Gary and Aunt Cynthia are standing. PHOTOGRAPH BY LES LEVERETT.

Throughout my life, he has enabled me to see things that others could not, or would not, notice. I am not the straight-ahead realistic artist that he is. I describe myself and my work as more abstract. I do not color within the lines, although I am capable of doing so. Daddy and I share an admiration for each other and our separate styles and laugh at our similarities. It's odd, but our photographs look related.

He never forced me to dream his dreams, but it was only natural that some of his became mine.

He set me on my course to play among the stars.

Dot, Les, and Libby Leverett in Goodlettsville. PHOTOGRAPHER UNKNOWN.

A PEARL IN A
SEA OF STARS

My childhood was rather different from the norm. Raised by a photographer in the music industry and a very creative mother, we had numerous friends and acquaintances from many different walks of life. They were constantly in and out of our home, and we were in and out of theirs. There was never a dull moment. Growing up in the sixties, I had two teenage brothers and every member of my immediate and extended family had a wonderfully relentless sense of humor.

Back in those days, most families' schedules and subsequent lives revolved around the "breadwinner's" work schedule. My friends mostly had very regimented lives. Everything was orderly and predictable. They got up at the same time every day. They ate breakfast, walked out the door, and returned at the same time day after day. Their families sat down to eat dinner when father arrived home from work in the evenings. They had bedtimes, which they stuck to like clockwork. They visited family on Saturday. Everyone went to church together on Sunday. Laundry was done on Monday.

I had one friend, Cindy, whose father worked the night shift for DuPont. Even though that meant the timing was different, the whole family still revolved around when her father was home or not, and they followed a set routine. They had to be quiet when they came in from school because he was sleeping. He woke for dinner and after a board game or two, he was off to work and they were off to bed. He woke them in the mornings, saw them off to school, and then the pattern started all over again.

My Dad's work schedule was hardly a schedule at all. Weekends were spent as the photographer for the *Grand Ole Opry*, and during the week, he worked for the National Life and Accident Insurance Company, the *Opry's* parent company, as head of the photography department. In addition, he moonlighted, taking publicity photographs and shots of local music industry events. It felt like he was always coming and going, always busy.

I was glad to see him come home. He would call to alert Mom that he was on his way and sometimes would get a grocery list from her and stop to pick up a few things for dinner. I usually met him in the driveway with a big hug. I remember how cool he would feel in the summer from having the car air conditioner on full blast. He always smelled of photographic chemicals. His tie would be hanging, untied from his neck, and it was usually stained from accidentally dipping it into the print developing trays. Mom was never happy over the condition of his ties. He would hug me up, ask me about my day, and say something like, "You're browner than a brown berry," referring to my tan. I was happy when Dad came home from work, but I was even happier to go to work with him, especially on Saturday nights when he had to work at the *Opry*. And expecially on *Opry* nights when Minnie Pearl was scheduled on the show.

There could be no darkness in a room when Minnie Pearl was present. She was luminous. Energy radiated from her big smile, and everyone wanted to be in its glow. She spread that glow by way of the *Grand Ole Opry*, which traveled over the airwaves into states I had never seen. Daddy used to listen to the *Opry* as a young boy in southern Alabama. He never dreamed that one day he would live in Nashville, much less that the *Opry* would be paying his bills.

The *Opry* paid the bills of many entertainers, announcers, musicians, and comedians, such as Minnie Pearl. If Roy Acuff was the "King of Country Music," then Minnie Pearl was the "Queen of Country Comedy."

Onstage or off, the jokes rolled off Minnie Pearl's tongue so naturally it made me wonder just what kind of childhood someone so funny, yet so sensitive, could have had. Did everyone in her family, like in mine, joke around all the time, or was her life pretty much normal?

The Ryman Auditorium in 1962. Photograph by Les Leverett.

One of the fringe benefits of Daddy's job was travel. My mother was more than willing to go to work with him on those assignments. She would plan and pack for weeks, and I loved watching her try on dresses she would be wearing to fancy dinners while on the trips. They traveled to exciting cities in America and visited many tropical locations and European countries. They sent postcards home to me (and the lucky babysitter of the week) and they all read, "P.S.: I hope you can see this place one day." Daddy always wanted to share his adventures. I guess that's why he was so interested in photography.

Minnie Pearl, Jim Nabors, and Libby backstage at the Ryman in 1970. PHOTOGRAPH BY LES LEVERETT.

One summer day, not long after I came into the world in 1960, Daddy was shopping during his lunch break at a department store in downtown Nashville and ran smack dab into Minnie Pearl. She wanted to know all the news and how the rest of the family was doing. She asked about Mom. When Dad told her that I had arrived, he said she acted like no other child had ever been born and it was the best news that she had heard in all her life. She threw her arms up in the air in an explosion of loud laughter and joy, followed with a hug. Knowing Minnie, I'm sure that it stopped the store momentarily. She was so loud and boisterous. I can just see her in one of these modes. Her arms went up, she threw back her head in a wide-mouthed laugh, then bent over and put her hands on her closed knees.

She was so personable and open. Daddy said that the first time he met her, she told him about how it was hard to be a female entertainer because, " . . . once a month a woman's got to go through 'that' and she just has to keep on going, no matter how bad she feels." Daddy felt rather surprised to be talking "female business" with someone he had just met, especially back in those days when bodily functions were dealt with more discreetly.

I don't remember when I first met Minnie Pearl. She was just always there. I do remember that she always made me feel special. Her hands were small and soft when she'd lean over, take one of mine, and twirl me around backstage at the Ryman when I was small. She always had a smile and kind word for me. When she hugged me, that darn hat always hit me in the face, and I was afraid that I would smash the pretty, ruffled, eyelet lace trim around the neck of her dress.

I used to sit back and watch in awe as she visited with people. Sometimes, backstage, she would take her hat off and straighten her hair. It was done up in a French twist. She would take bobby pins out of it and, while holding the pins in her mouth, tuck some stray hairs back into the twist and then pin it up again. The hat would go back on and a couple of more pins would go back to hold it secure, doing all this while carrying on a conversation. She was so animated and delightful. She'd pass out hugs, then throw those arms up in the air, then her hands would go on her knees, with the quake of roaring laughter all around her. It was just so predictable. She would then kiss everyone on her way out. Although she never wore lipstick, you felt like you had a big smooch mark on your cheek. It was like an invisible sign that she left behind that said, "Minnie was here." I proudly wore that sign many times.

Once, when I was a young teenager, I ran into her somewhere other than the Ryman. For some ridiculous reason, I thought that she would not recognize me. (Had puberty really done that much damage?) Maybe I feared that everything stable and constant in my life was going away, including the people that I had grown up around. It was a very age-appropriate thought, I guess. I said, "I don't know if you remember me, but I'm Libby, Les's daughter." She threw her head back and laughed. She hugged me tight, planted a big smooch on my cheek and said, "Why, of course I remember you!" She smiled that smile, that understanding, loving smile, and I cannot tell you how reassuring that was to me in my adolescence.

I always felt as if I could really just sit down and have a heart-to-heart girl talk with her, but I never did. If I had, maybe I could have asked her that question I had always wondered . . . What was her childhood really like? What seed was planted that made her so doggone funny?

In her skits, she often spoke of her early days in fictional "Grinder's Switch." Grinder's Switch wasn't really the name of a town, but a railroad switchyard. She fashioned "Grinder's Switch" after her nearby hometown of Centerville, Tennessee. Her upbringing sounded as southern and simple as you could get. Some of the characters in her act she made up and some she supposedly knew in her youth. They had simple minds, and her descriptions of these characters were part of what made her act so darn funny. (*"Junior was so cockeyed that he could stand on the front porch and count the chickens in the backyard."*) She must have had many friends as a child.

I also grew up in a small, simple town. Goodlettsville, Tennessee, is a suburb of Nashville. It was close enough to the city that we could find culture, yet far enough out of the hubbub to be safe. Although I seemed like any other kid in our neighborhood, I was living a different and, in its own way, a charmed life. I don't mean private schools and nice material things, but something that cannot be bought, only experienced.

And experiences, I've had many. I tagged along with my Daddy to sit among writers, actors, stunt men, artists, dancers, instrument makers, singers, performers, and producers as they turned up their coffee cups into the wee hours of the morning and shared their latest experiences and their deepest thoughts and dreams.

I would sit in front of fireplaces, hang out on staircases, and fall asleep in corners and on couches in homes, offices, and studios of people who were great, thought they were great, or dreamed of greatness.

You never knew who would show up at our house. Music folks would drop in at all times of the night with Krispy Kreme doughnuts in one hand and a guitar case in the other. Mom would put the coffee on, and the conversation would fly until the early hours of morning. I'd lie in my bed and listen.

The discussions that the adults were having and bits and pieces of stories would inspire me in ways I could not imagine back then. I heard hit songs in their infancy, songs that people would eventually sing along with while listening to their radio. I heard road stories from entertainers and sad tales of failure, rejection, and broken dreams.

I watched and listened as Daddy worked and played with these creative people. I watched his easygoing style, his way of making people feel comfortable and then snapping their photograph while they were unaware. His timing was perfect. He knew just when to let that shutter go right after a blink or at the height of a toothy smile. He was a smooth operating photographer. His photos vouched for this. Even when not working, when just hanging around with these interesting people, he was "on." Always quick with wit and pranks, always a true friend, no one loved a good laugh more than Daddy did . . . unless it was Minnie.

"Tour buses," "managers," "demos," "contracts," "sessions," "engagements," "photo shoots," "openings," and other topics my friends never heard of were common subjects in the circles I found myself.

I fell asleep at school all the time. My teachers must have thought this was terrible. Little did they know that I was getting an education of my own, something that could not be taught in a classroom. *Captain Kangaroo* would make me feel good and happy, but he didn't fill my head with dreams the way these experiences did.

My late nights at these people's homes, in recording studios, at plays and shows, and TV tapings and openings, fueled my love of the arts and gave me a better sense of the important things in life at a very early age. I also learned who to follow and who I should not be around.

Minnie Pearl was definitely a leader, and her example was one to be followed (with the exception of a few of her jokes, which I was not supposed to have overheard). She had a heart of gold and would do anything at all to help anyone in need. Her greatest mission though, was bringing joy through laughter. She would do her comedy routine, which was sprinkled with enough poignancy to make everyone feel connected and leave the audience laughing.

On many occasions I would go bopping into a dressing room at the Ryman where she had people gathered around her, obviously telling a joke. Sometimes the room would go quiet, and everyone would turn and look at me in a way that said, "Go away kid, so we can hear the punch line to this nasty joke!" I got the message and left. Every now and then, I would go just outside the door so I could still hear.

I rarely saw her alone. There always seemed to be a small crowd of people trying to get in on the glow. If laughter is the best medicine, then Minnie Pearl was a walking apothecary of healing goods.

Clowns have never appealed to me. They seem frightening and strange. I never figured out why someone thought that clowns would

Backstage at the Opry House in 1979 in Roy Acuff's dressing room. Minnie Pearl has just told a good joke. (l to r) Minnie, Roy, Jeanne Pruett, and Ben Smathers of the Stoney Mountain Cloggers. PHOTOGRAPH BY LES LEVERETT.

cheer someone up with all that paint on their faces and loud noise-makers. However, if clowns came in the kind of package that Minnie Pearl presented, that would be different.

Just looking at her would bring giggles. She always wore a gingham dress and a hat with the price tag still on it. Her shoes had taps attached to the toes, so you could always hear her coming. If you didn't hear the taps, you would hear the laughter that followed her. It spread over her audience like sunlight. Indeed, when Minnie Pearl was around, there was sunshine.

I went to her house several times with my daddy when he took photos of her. She lived in Nashville on Curtiswood Lane next door to the governor's mansion. My head bobbed back and forth as we drove into her

Minnie Pearl on a stairway in her home on Curtiswood Lane in 1975. PHOTOGRAPH BY LES LEVERETT.

neighborhood. The neatly manicured lawns and fountains and pools and huge houses were beyond my childhood dreams. We lived in a middle-class neighborhood, and I always gawked when we walked into her home. It was like something out of a storybook with a curved staircase and tennis courts out back. Fine art hung on the walls, and it was as quiet as a museum. There were no children to dictate a primary color scheme in this house. Instead, she had dogs, fluffy, little yappy lap dogs, which I dearly loved. They were totally devoted to Minnie, so I never got much of a chance to play with them.

Minnie Pearl was transformed into Mrs. Sarah Cannon at her home. Gone was the country gingham dress and straw hat. In their place would be a pastel colored suit and instead of black Mary Janes with taps, she wore heels. Her hair would be done up nicely on top of her head and she wore nice jewelry. Sheer hose replaced the thick white tights that she wore with her stage clothes. When she walked into the foyer to greet us, she would have a grin on her face, like she knew that I was shocked and that I did not expect her to look so classy. Something about Mrs. Cannon that never changed was her radiance.

Minnie answered her own door, and after a time of visiting and catching up on the news, Dad would start bringing out his camera equipment. Minnie would ask my dad, "Les, where do you want me?" Then they'd both burst into laughter. Laughter, always laughter. I remember one portrait that Dad took of Minnie on her grand staircase. They worked and worked on getting her hands in the right place to look natural. She would be looking just right, Daddy would say something funny, she would crack up laughing, and they would have to start over again. Daddy would take her hand and lead her down the steps, like a true gentleman. The women always adored my handsome, polite dad.

I watched. I listened. I learned.

Mrs. Cannon's husband, Henry, was rarely seen in public. I honestly don't remember him speaking much beyond a friendly, soft, "hello" and a nod of his head. Once, he said to me, "My you've grown." I believe that was the longest chat I ever had with Mr. Cannon. Yes, Mr. Cannon. I never called him Henry but always called his wife Minnie. Oddly, I don't recall seeing him in his own home but maybe once, and I know I did not see him at the *Opry* more than a handful of times. It was so rare, that when he did show up, Dad or Minnie always felt like they had to reintroduce him to me. Dad used to say, "This is Mr. Minnie Pearl," and everyone around us, including Mr. Cannon would laugh. He would stand in the shadows backstage, and if anyone wanted to visit with him, they had to find him, and they usually did. He attracted people just like Minnie. Oh, did Minnie love her Henry! She usually mentioned him in her set. He was her personal pilot and flew her to her out-of-town engagements.

The Cannons had a guesthouse where people like Jim Nabors would stay while in town. I was thrilled to have met him on many occasions dur-

Jim Nabors performing on the *Opry* show at the Ryman in 1970. Minnie Pearl is in the background to the left; Spider Wilson and Ralph Davis are playing. Archie Campbell is standing behind the piano (with his arm on top). PHOTOGRAPH BY LES LEVERETT.

ing my childhood but could never get used to calling him Mr. Nabors. He was always "Gomer Pyle" to me. His television characters were so silly and none too bright. Backstage, though, he was so different. He was always well dressed and looked very debonair. When he sang, it was a shock. Everyone expected, "Gooooolly" and instead, out came a deep, smooth, operatic, voice.

Many times I would hear Minnie Pearl perform on the stage at the Opry House with Roy Acuff. They seemed to go together like fried chicken and a picnic. If you saw one of them, the other was nearby. Mr. Acuff had the ability to woo crowds and entertain the masses with his "Wabash Cannonball." He could do wonders with the fiddle. He could even balance his fiddle on top of his bow, which was balanced on the tip

Minnie and Roy performing in 1978. Ralph Davis is on the left. PHOTOGRAPH BY LES LEVERETT.

of his nose. This was very magical to me, but even more magical was the chemistry between him and Minnie. They would play off each other's jokes on stage, and it would make the crowd roar with laughter. I was told that it was never rehearsed.

Minnie's trademark greeting was, "Howdy, I'm just so proud to be here!" Actually, that was a long, drawn out, "How-deeee" with a pause, which was usually reciprocated by her audiences with loud applause, laughter, and sometimes, if the crowd was lively, a "How-deeee" in return. Then, "I'm just so proud to be here!" She usually went right into a joke or story. ("*How-deee, I'm just so proud to be here. The other day I was down at Uncle Nabob's smokehouse when it occurred to me that I had not seen that pet pig of his for some time. . . .*")

Roy Acuff, Minnie Pearl, and Boxcar Willie in 1979. PHOTOGRAPH BY LES LEVERETT.

Many people have goofed up our name over the years. The spelling was hard enough, especially after we learned that one branch of the family had added an E to the end. Leverett is British and means baby hare. I guess that's why the vet laughed when Mom called him on behalf of my sick pet bunny and gave him our name. Our family crest has three hares jumping gracefully around the borders. Dad joked that it was a great name since our family reproduced like a bunch of rabbits.

We got letters addressed to everything from "Levit" to "Lenerett." Dad once got a letter at his office addressed to "Chef Photog" where they had given up on Leverett and just decided to goof up "Chief Photographer." Even Daddy's Grammy award had his named spelled with an E on the end. Oh, how many times have I heard and used the phrase, "Leverett. Just like Everett, but with an L in front." Well, Grandpa Jones's wife, Ramona, always used a plural version of our name. Backstage, she would introduce Dad to her friends with, "This is Les Leveretts." She knew me as "Libby Leveretts." Roy Acuff always called Dad "Les Levert" with a French twist to it. But Minnie, well, she never got the part about, "with an L in front." She always knew us as the Everett family. She mailed Dad postcards, did business with him, heard his name over and over backstage, and saw it in print constantly. I'm sure she wrote a couple of checks with our name, but we still remained, the "Everetts." I figure that to find Dad's name in her telephone book, she had to look in the Es. That always seemed so odd to me. She knew my dad for the last forty years of her life, but she still didn't get it right.

It all came back to me though, one night, when I was grown and running around backstage at the Opry House, with my own camera in tow, working myself silly on a tight schedule. I always stopped to chat with the people I knew and loved, no matter how busy I was. I learned that from Dad. He never forgot the best part of being a photographer in the music industry was the people. I was particularly busy this evening and on my way through the performers' lounge, or green room, as it was fondly called. I saw Minnie, and she saw me at the same time. We hugged, and she asked about Daddy and wondered where he was. She had a gleam in her eyes like she was happy to see me following in his footsteps. Our conversation was short, and I excused myself to go take a photo on the stage.

When I returned, a slight, rather handsome man and his friend approached me and said they noticed me talking to Minnie Pearl. They wanted to know how I knew her and if I would introduce them to her and snap a photo for them. Well, I pride myself in having great people skills, but I really goofed up when I forgot to ask this man and his friend what their names were. I dragged them over to where Minnie had just finished

k.d.lang at Fan Fair in Nashville in 1986. PHOTOGRAPH BY LIBBY LEVERETT-CREW.

a conversation with someone else and proceeded to introduce her. Well, I realized that I had never called her anything but Minnie, or Minnie Pearl. Suddenly, I felt like I should be more respectful and added a Mrs. After stumbling around with it, I said, "Mrs. Pearl, these young men have asked me to introduce you to them. This is . . . ," my mind was blank. I had forgotten to ask for their names. The young man and his companion held out their hands and gave Minnie their names, which I didn't hear because I was so flustered. I snapped a quick photo for them and once again had to leave the conversation to go work. I chuckled at myself all night thinking about how I had goofed up Minnie's name. If I was going to use "Mrs.," it should have been "Mrs. Cannon," for Pete's sake!

The next morning, I was telling my husband about my faux pas. About that time, he held up the newspaper he was reading with a huge ad for a new female singer named k.d. lang and said, "Wow, she looks just like a man!" I glanced over and almost choked. That was the "young man" I had introduced to Minnie the night before. It was no wonder they looked at me strangely. I thought they were just wondering why I had goofed up Minnie's name if I knew her so well.

k.d. lang went on to make a name for herself in the music industry. She has a wonderful voice, and I've always hoped that she wasn't too upset that I goofed up her gender. Maybe my introducing her to "Mrs. Pearl" made up for it.

I never asked Minnie if she realized the error that night, or if so, when she realized my mistake. Maybe it was when she, too, read the paper the next day. I'm sure that she had a good belly laugh if she did, and no one would appreciate such a blunder as much as her.

Minnie Pearl was not all laughs at all times, although to her audience, that must have been what it seemed. I had seen her almost in tears, talking about Roy Acuff. She loved him so much. She made it clear that if he died before she did, she would never be back to perform on the stage of the *Grand Ole Opry*.

Roy Acuff died on a dreary autumn day in November of 1992, and I

Roy and Minnie together at the Opry in 1978. This is Libby's favorite photograph of them. PHOTOGRAPH BY LES LEVERETT.

never saw Minnie's glow at the Opry House again, although I would always feel it.

The last time I saw Minnie, I was photographing a convention in Nashville, and she was performing as their evening's entertainment. She was fabulous. It was the longest set I had ever seen her do, since most of her performances on the *Opry* were short, less than fifteen minutes or so. As usual, she told stories from her childhood, stories of acquaintances and friends, characters so familiar to her fans. She shared sad stories of broken hearts and lost loved ones, then moved everyone into a steady stream of humor, song, and laughter. I could see Mr. Cannon standing behind the stage. After this performance, I felt that I could fly. I really felt just that high and uplifted. I tried to make my way over to visit with her, but the crowd around her was too thick. I figured that I would catch up with her one day . . . somewhere else.

The news of her death in 1996 broke my heart. It had been hard enough getting used to not seeing her at the Opry House, now to never see her again. It was just too sad.

"There goes the greatest guitar player in the world and we, around here, take him for granted; we forget how great he is" she said to Dad one night while standing backstage watching Chet Atkins receive a standing ovation.

Dad replied, "It's the same with you, Minnie! You're great too, and we take you for granted. You are loved by people all over the world!"

"Ah, go on!" was her humble reply.

"You could tell the same jokes every time, but they always sound fresh and new because you have such good timing with your humor."

"Ah, go on, Les!"

"Minnie, I love you!"

I'm sure there was a hug and big smooch, followed by laughter, of course.

Minnie was here. And we're so proud she was.

THE MOTHER CHURCH
AND GRANDPA

Something about the sun going down, knowing it was Saturday, and the fact that my hair had been up in rollers for a good part of the afternoon made me excited with the anticipation that I would be going to work with my daddy.

The energy in our home on those nights was strong. Mom would be in the kitchen making our usual Saturday night meal of hamburgers, Daddy would be in the shower causing the scent of Dial soap to waft through the house, and in the back corner of our dwelling, the walls of my brothers' room were throbbing with the sounds of Jimi Hendrix or the Grateful Dead. We would rush through dinner, make sure lights were left on, and all the windows were closed and locked. Daddy usually made sure all of his equipment was in order for his long night of work. Last thing, Mom would take the rollers out of my hair and brush it into loose banana curls that usually didn't make it through the night. She always made sure I was dressed as cute as could be when I went to work with Daddy.

The music at the Ryman was country, about as country as you could get. So, I'd have a big dose of country on the weekend followed by smaller doses of '60s rock 'n' roll via my teenage brothers, sprinkled with classical and big band jazz over the family radio throughout the week.

I loved going to work with my daddy at the Ryman Auditorium. Butterflies danced in my stomach all the way from the suburbs into the city. I could see the lights and traffic and hustle bustle of people going places. People from other towns, other states, and other countries would come to the *Grand Ole Opry*. Although I didn't know why and may never know why, even then I knew it was something special and I was in the very middle of it.

You could hear the music before we even stepped out of our Pontiac. You could hear not one song, but several. Not just from the Ryman, but from all of the clubs around the Ryman and on Broadway.

I had heard of Tootsie's Orchid Lounge, and it was always flavored with laughter and a bit of naughtiness like it was some place that was fun, but you shouldn't go and if you did, you shouldn't let anyone see you there. Its back door was so close to the backstage door of the Ryman that I guess the artists and other musicians felt almost obligated to drop in.

Daddy always made me stay close to him in the parking lot and in the alley behind the majestic brick building. I was right with him as we made our way up the narrow stairs to the backstage door. People always hung out there; autograph seekers, fans, people who had journeyed from afar to meet the country star of their dreams. They would reach for us and ask Daddy questions, and he would hurry through them, yet I never saw him treat any of them rudely.

The smell of cigarette smoke, perfume, and sweat in the summer, wafted out the door and flowed down the stairway to greet all who passed by. To most, the smell must have been nasty, but to me, it was just the Ryman. It was familiar and comforting and carried with it the hope of a new adventure.

Mr. Bell was the guard at the backstage door in those days. He made sure that everyone who showed up was supposed to be there, and I suppose he had orders from some parents to make sure that their children didn't go back out. I never saw him without a clipboard. On this clipboard were the names of each entertainer who was performing for the night, their musicians, and maybe a few of their guests. He checked everyone's name off as they came and went. I guess those guys who went over to Tootsie's had several check marks by their names. I don't recall our name ever being on the list in the early days. Daddy was a fixture at the Ryman.

Everyone loved Daddy not only because he was a kind, funny person but also because his photos were important to them. Not only did his photos promote music careers, they were also a way to record history. And a lot of history was made at the Ryman.

Daddy had his bag of cameras and film and he often asked me to help him carry his equipment. He had a telephoto lens that was almost as long as I was tall, and when I carried it for him, it was heavy and awkward, but it made me proud. When Mom was with us, Daddy would stash smaller lenses in her purse, and she made jokes that it was the reason he carried her along with him.

The backstage area of the Ryman was small and crowded, and navigating was not easy for a small child. Most of the time, I liked to find a perch to sit and "people watch."

I always met the most unexpected personalities at the *Opry*. You just never knew who would show up there.

Alisa Jones, Libby Leverett, Alcyon Beasley, DeFord Bailey, and his biographer, David C. Morton, on the stage of the Ryman in 1974. PHOTOGRAPH BY LES LEVERETT.

Willie Nelson backstage at the Ryman in 1965. Libby is closing her eyes in anticipation of the flash. PHOTOGRAPH BY LES LEVERETT.

What I really liked though was the regular parade of stardom that passed through the narrow backstage hallways of the Ryman. I liked the way the fancy cowboy boots and high heels clicked on the squeaky wood floors. I liked the smells of popcorn and the busy sounds of music and laughter that I found backstage. And the crowd's applause filled me with joy.

A typical crowd at the Ryman Auditorium. PHOTOGRAPH BY LES LEVERETT.

While Daddy was working, I had firm orders not to go outside, out into the audience, or to stage right. Stage right was more or less where all the men hung out in their small dressing rooms. I guess the language was too rough or the jokes too crude. Instead, I would linger around the mailroom backstage. The mailroom doubled as a break room and a path from the backstage area to the front or audience area of the Ryman. If I wanted a Coke or popcorn, I had to get an adult to go out front with me. In the winter, when that door into the audience opened, a big puff of cold air came in from a nearby exterior front door.

I loved to go out front. There were so many people, and they all looked so happy. Daddy would hustle through the crowds with me in tow, camera equipment hanging off both shoulders. He would take out a battered leather wallet and pay for my treats, then take me backstage again so he could do his job.

Sometimes, if he had to grab a quick photo while out front, he would take me down in front of the stage with him. The entertainers would often acknowledge Daddy with a nod of the head or smile, or with a "There's our photographer working hard tonight folks." The audience would look at Daddy, he would bow or wave in a funny manner, and I would feel a rush of pride that swept over me and made my face turn red. How I adored my daddy.

An enthusiastic audience at the Ryman Auditorium. PHOTOGRAPH BY LES LEVERETT.

Backstage, I spent endless time with Alisa, one of my best friends whose father was an entertainer named Grandpa Jones. It seemed we had been friends longer than we could remember. Our parents were good friends, and the Joneses lived near our home in the suburbs. At that time, they lived on a steep hill and I loved going to their place just for the thrill of that driveway.

We lived on the way to the Ryman, and sometimes the Joneses would drop Alisa off at our house when Alisa and I would choose to stay home with my mom. Her parents and Daddy would go on to work. Mom's hair would be up in rollers. She would read her Sunday school lesson as the *Grand Ole Opry* played on the radio. We would play with Barbies and listen. With the radio on, we felt like we hadn't missed a thing.

Libby and Alisa backstage in the mailroom/lounge at the Ryman in 1971.
PHOTOGRAPH BY LES LEVERETT.

Alisa and I would sometimes bring grocery bags full of Barbies and all their clothing to play with on those long Saturday nights that we chose to spend at the Ryman. We sat at sticky little café tables in front of the stars' mailboxes. They would often stop to visit with us when they came to check their mail, and many times we would have to move so they could get to their box. Around the top of this backstage area was a display of the *Opry* members' photos. They were backlit and bright and some of them, like Grandpa Jones's, had faded over time. Every single one of them had been taken by my daddy.

The photographs around the backstage area of the Ryman. PHOTOGRAPH BY LES LEVERETT.

In those days, Grandpa wore gray pinstripe pants, red suspenders, a long-sleeve shirt, tall leather boots, and a floppy leather hat. He wore a rhinestone pin on his suspenders that said, "CA." I still do not know exactly what it stood for. (As close as Alisa and I were, she never would tell me. Daddy knows and still isn't telling.) He had a pasted-on mustache, gray spray in his hair, and the lines on his face were drawn on. It gave me the creeps, and I always wondered why they called him "Grandpa" when he wasn't one.

As the years went by, Grandpa eventually grew his own gray hair and mustache, and with all that laughing his face became etched with wrinkles. He was probably the only man ever to be glad of it.

Grandpa Jones at the studio in Nashville in 1961. PHOTOGRAPH BY LES LEVERETT.

Everybody called him "Grandpa," and I mean everybody. Through the fame of *Hee Haw*, which was a syndicated television show, he became "Everybody's Grandpa." Because of one regular skit on this show, people came up to him all the time and asked, "Hey Grandpa, what's for supper?" In the skit, he would be looking out of a country kitchen window, and he would answer with something like, "Venison roast with onion and taters, with a good-size bowl of okra and tomatoes, homemade light bread a golden brown, and the strongest coffee there is around."

Bill Carlisle and George McCormick sharing a laugh with Grandpa Jones backstage at the Opry in 1978. PHOTOGRAPH BY LES LEVERETT.

Grandpa Jones on the set of the video for *A Christmas Guest* in East Tennessee in 1991. PHOTOGRAPH BY LIBBY LEVERETT-CREW.

He was a character. It seemed that everything he said was funny, and his slow country voice just made it funnier. His hearing was bad, and because of this, part of his humor came from miscommunication. I can just hear him now, "Eh? Whajasay?" (Huh, What did you say?)

When I grew up, they did a video of Grandpa's poem *A Christmas Guest*. The video crew, the Jones family, the production crew, the actors, and extras were on location in East Tennessee at the Museum of Appalachia. I was part of the production crew, shooting the still photographs. We had spent a long, cold yet magical, fun day of filming. Alisa's husband, Ron, remarked that if it snowed and they could turn off the

51

snow machine, he would go to church on Sunday. Well, all of a sudden, it began snowing, and Ramona, his wife, told him to get his suit ready. It was as cold as could be, and even under layers of clothing my teeth were chattering. I thought my cameras would freeze up. The crew was preparing a scene, and I sought out the warmth of the fireplace, which happened to have drawn Grandpa for the same reason. It was quiet there, and we both had our backsides to the fire, not talking, just relaxing. Out of the blue silence Grandpa said, "Eh? Whajasay?" I looked at him rather startled and replied, "I didn't say anything, Grandpa." He said, "Wheel, I have to ast ever now and then just to make sure."

When I asked him once what his son, Mark, was doing, his reply was, "Not a dern thing and he doesn't start that 'til a noon."

When we were very small, Alisa and I were playing outside at their house while our moms visited and Daddy shot some publicity photos of Grandpa. Our game of the hour was trying to catch their wild cat. It ran for its life and led us through a lot of dirt and poison ivy, but we finally caught her on top of their picnic table. Grandpa saw us and yelled, "Wheel, don't go mashin' the cat!" Everyone cracked up.

Alisa and Libby at the Jones's in 1965. PHOTOGRAPH BY LES LEVERETT.

The interesting thing about Grandpa was that although he was fun-loving, he was very moody, and he had a hot temper.

Daddy tells the story about how Grandpa and a mutual friend of theirs were riding in Grandpa's station wagon. A storm "came a brewin'" and Grandpa turned the windshield wipers on. They didn't work. It was raining so hard that he couldn't see to drive. He beat on the windshield wiper switch to no avail, pulled over in a huff, got out in the rain and climbed onto the hood of the car. He grabbed both of the blades, swished them back and forth, and yelled, "This is the way you do it!"

Ramona, Alisa, and her three older siblings just grinned a knowing grin when Grandpa would go off. I think they knew when to just stay out of his way, and when the going got tough, the tough went shopping. Ramona and Alisa loved to shop.

With Grandpa's hearing problem, he talked and laughed very loudly. Sometimes it would frighten me when I was little. He would show up in that little mailroom backstage at the Ryman, his banjo attached to a strap around his neck and always laughing. We always knew where he was, and wherever he was, so was his banjo.

When we became a little older, Alisa and I were allowed to climb the old, creaky steps to the balcony on the side stage at the Ryman. When we were little, Alisa was a tomboy. She would wear shorts and cowboy boots. Her hair was cut short in a pixie hairdo, and she loved catching salamanders, which I helped her sell backstage to the men who fished with them. As I mentioned before, my mom always made sure I was dressed cute and my hair ribbons matched my dress every time I went out the door. I wore ruffled, lacy panties until I was in third grade.

By the time Alisa and I were permitted to venture away from that mailroom backstage, our dress codes were beginning to shift. We had both become tomboys. I exchanged ruffled panties for elephant leg jeans and Peter Max sweatshirts. Alisa and I both wore our "maxi-length" coats, no matter how hot it was, to cover our growing/changing bodies. (In later years the shift came back full circle. Alisa was never seen without

D. J. Jim Kizzia (KBIX, Muskogee, Oklahoma) visiting with Paul Warren and Cousin Jake Tullock (Flatt and Scruggs's musicians) and Les Leverett at the Ryman in 1965. FROM THE COLLECTION OF LES LEVERETT.

makeup, and her clothes were feminine and refined. I, on the other hand, could skip the makeup thing completely, and my idea of a fine dress would be a frumpy, cotton one, with Teva sandals or tennis shoes.)

We would giggle and "people watch" up in the balcony, sitting in style in our hip huggers, and sweating to death with those big winter coats on. From where we sat, we could see the whole backstage area, separated from the stage by the giant canvas backdrops that said things like "Martha White" and "Purina Dog Chow." They were sponsors of the *Grand Ole Opry,* and their products were hawked between acts, by the same announcers who waved their hands in the air to get the audience to applaud at the end of each song.

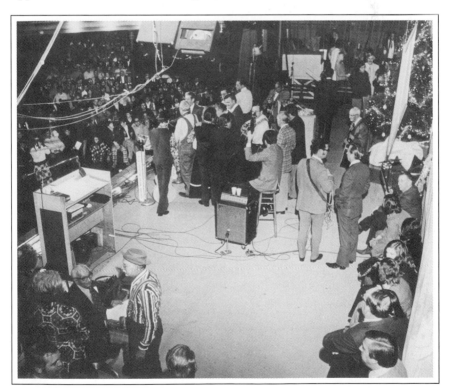

From the balcony looking down on the backstage at the Ryman during one of Roy Acuff's performances in 1973. Grandpa Jones is in the left corner talking with Vito Pellettieri, *Opry* stage manager at the time. PHOTOGRAPH BY LES LEVERETT.

From the balcony looking down on the backstage at the Ryman of one of Flatt and Scruggs's performances in 1971. PHOTOGRAPH BY LES LEVERETT.

Beyond the stage was the crowd, fanning, fanning, fanning, and clapping. They always looked so hot and sweaty. Most nights, there was such a crowd that the people were jammed up against each other and the balcony was crowded all the way to where the rope blocked off the restricted backstage balcony. They didn't sell tickets for that area because you had to look through a web of pulleys and ropes and backdrops to see the stage, or anything else for that matter. I didn't care if I really couldn't see that well; I was just there for the adventure, and ropes and crowds added to it. It never crossed my mind that the people on the

Grandpa's family in 1979: (l to r), Eloise, Alisa, Ramona, unidentified bassist, Grandpa, Marsha, and Mark. PHOTOGRAPH BY LES LEVERETT.

other side of that line in the balcony would love to have had a glimpse of the backstage area of the Ryman into which I had been born.

On nights when a great crowd was expected, they would take down the rope and fill the balcony to capacity. I wasn't allowed to go up there on those evenings.

Sometimes we would catch Grandpa's act from up there. His act was high energy and funny. He played banjo and sang as Ramona played fiddle and sang with him. They did a lot of the old standard folk tunes.

During the Christmas season, Grandpa would perform with cowbells tied to his ankles while holding handbells, in each hand. Ramona would also play handbells, and together they'd run through a medley of favorite Christmas tunes. *Jingle Bells*, of course was the big hit. Grandpa switched legs to ring different bells, and he looked like a marionette puppet. It was like a little dance.

There were other dancers on the *Opry*, a group of about three or four couples who would square dance between sets. The women would have on short, twirly dresses and the men wore matching shirts. They all had loud taps on their shoes, but the stage technicians would always lay micro-phones on the floor to enhance the sound. The dancers' legs would be moving so fast you couldn't see them.

The Stoney Mountain Cloggers performing on the Ryman stage. PHOTOGRAPH BY LES LEVERETT.

When all the excitement in the balcony or in the mailroom got to be too much, we would go visit James and Rosa. They were the people who kept the backstage area clean and supplied with coffee and lemonade. Daddy always drank coffee as the night wore on and it got late. I remember him swinging through the mailroom to check on me some nights backstage. He would hug or kiss me on the head and his breath smelled of coffee. On any given Saturday night, I could drink my weight in lemonade. James and Rosa would see me coming and have a cup waiting.

I would visit and they would keep refilling. Alisa was rather quiet, so I, who have never had trouble finding something to say, usually visited a while. The contrast between Rosa's very dark skin and her crisp white uniform was lovely. I liked to watch her gracefully pour cup upon cup of lemonade and line them up in neat little rows on the serving table for backstage visitors. James didn't sit much. He always seemed to be on the run, delivering supplies, cleaning up other peoples' messes, and tending to his other duties. Sweat was always dripping down his face, but he always had a kind word and a smile. When he did sit, he always leaned back in his chair, on two legs, and he clasped his arms behind his head as he talked.

As Rosa aged, her hair turned as white as her uniform, giving her a regal glow. She is a lovely woman. Many nights after the *Opry*, Jerry Strobel, the Opry House manager at the time, would give Rosa a ride home so she wouldn't have to ride the city bus late at night.

One night, when I was older, Daddy wasn't feeling well. He really needed to get a photo but just didn't think he could make it. The person whose photo he needed was not scheduled to perform until one of the last sets. I felt like I had arrived when he asked if I would take the photo for him. It was as though I had been turned loose with the car and trusted to drive to California and back. He left his camera with me, arranged for Jerry to take me home, and he went on home to rest.

Although I was always sociable, I remember not knowing what I should talk about with Jerry. He had a real old car and made a few jokes about it, and he asked me about school. He understood kids since he had a houseful, so he didn't mind my disjointed conversation skills. A couple of years later, Jerry's car finally quit for good, and on the back of the *Opry* program that weekend was a comical death notice for it.

I think Jerry had also given Grandpa a couple of rides home over the years. I don't think the conversation on those trips was as strained as mine was with him. Jerry, like the rest of the world, loved to hear Grandpa talk.

The Opry duck hunt in 1994, taken at Reelfoot Lake in Samburg, Tennessee. (l to r) Bud Wendell, Les Leverett, unidentified guide, Dr. Perry Harris, Grandpa Jones, unidentified guide/writer, Bob Whitaker, Neil Craig, Stu Phillips, Little Jimmy Dickens, Charlie Walker, unidentified guide, Jim Ed Brown, unidentified guide, Sonny Cochran, a guide, and Jimmy C. Newman. FROM THE COLLECTION OF LES LEVERETT.

Grandpa was one of Daddy's favorite people. They shared many experiences together and grew close over the years.

For around twenty-five years, there was an annual *Opry* duck hunt. It was an exclusive club of men who were members of, or worked for, the *Opry*. They would meet up at the Ryman parking lot on a cold day the week after Christmas every year, and pile into a couple of vehicles or an RV and head off for a few days at Reelfoot Lake in West Tennessee. Every year they received a new memento of the trip that had the date and *Annual Grand Ole Opry Duck Hunt, Reelfoot Lake* inscribed on it. It was usually a camouflage item, such as a hat, down vest, or jacket. Everyone hunted, except Daddy. The only thing he ever shot were photographs, and he did a lot of that on these trips. The men went with the intention of duck hunting, but personally I think it was just a long "guys night out." Daddy always came home with hilarious stories of mishaps and a new batch of road tales from the entertainers. He also had several new jokes, some of which my ears will never hear.

On these duck hunts, Daddy always shared a room with Grandpa. It was a perfect roommate arrangement; Grandpa's hearing was so bad, Daddy's snoring didn't bother him, and Daddy loved Grandpa so much, he didn't mind his complaining and grumbling. As a matter of fact, I think Daddy liked it. It was just Grandpa doing what he did best . . . entertaining.

One of my favorite stories is about Vic Willis of the Willis Brothers. He was riding with Grandpa to Memphis for a show they both had to play. Grandpa was driving. Before they left Nashville, Vic put a sign on the back of the car that said, "Just Married." As they traveled down the interstate, Vic put his arm up on the back of the seat behind Grandpa and scooted over as close as he could. Grandpa asked, "Why do yeh reckon all these folks are a smilin' at us and a beepin'?" Vic told him it was because he was so famous and people were just recognizing him.

They would return from these trips in time to be at the *Opry* on

Grandpa Jones at Tut Taylor's office in 1974. PHOTOGRAPH BY LES LEVERETT.

Friday night, and for a good six months you could hear the same funny stories being told over and over again, most of them about something Grandpa said or did.

As with most good things, my Saturday nights at the *Opry* had to end. When my mom was with us, I would sometimes pull a chair up next to her and lay my head in her lap. Alisa would just lay her head on the table. Mom would gently smooth my now-flattened banana curls, and I would drift off to sleep listening to the rhythm of her voice talking with her friends, and in the background, the music from the stage.

Grandpa, Alisa, and Ramona leaving the Ryman in 1972. Note the cowbells under Grandpa's arm. PHOTOGRAPH BY LES LEVERETT.

Many Sunday mornings I would awaken, not remembering my daddy carrying me down the narrow backstage passageway into the alley behind the Ryman to our car. The trip home from the dark, quiet city was just a blur. Those Sunday mornings, I would lie there and remember my Saturday night at the *Opry*. I would think about the faces I saw, the people I met, the warmth of having a good friend like Alisa, the way my daddy worked and the security of having Mom chatting with the ladies backstage. The songs and Grandpa's banjo tunes would ring around in my head, laced with laughter and applause, and I knew, even then, that these were precious things.

A LONG, TALL TALE

At the top of the growth chart was Stringbean. His real name was David Akeman, but if you saw him, you knew why David just didn't fit. He was as tall and thin as a string bean. He had puppy dog eyes and his face was long and slender. He could play the fire out of a banjo, and when he smiled you saw every single tooth in his head. He was not only a wonderful player, he was also quite the comedian. This was obvious from the way he dressed at show time.

When Stringbean came in the backstage door at the Ryman Auditorium, he would have on overalls. Estelle, his wife, would stay in

Writer Bill Littleton interviewing Stringbean for *Performance* magazine backstage at the Ryman in 1971. PHOTOGRAPH BY LES LEVERETT.

Stringbean backstage at WSM-TV in 1961. PHOTOGRAPH BY LES LEVERETT.

the mailroom/lounge area, usually sitting with my mom. I remember her in large floral print dresses and cat's-eye glasses. She had a round face and a sweet smile. There would be much laughter and giggling. Most of the time I had to just wonder what they were talking about. They would visit the night away over a box of popcorn. The Akemans were simple folks. To the outsider, they would look very much like a farmer and wife who had just come in from slopping the pigs. Stringbean would mingle and laugh his way to the other side of the stage where the men's room was, and he would emerge sometime later in his stage wear. He was so tall he had to duck as he went through the narrow sloping hall going to the stage area.

Stringbean's character was all about his stage wear. He wore small long pants attached to a very long striped shirt. They were sewn together so it looked like he had very short legs and a very long torso. He wore cowboy boots and a silly hat that, combined with that toothy smile, was a sight to behold.

Like Stringbean, some entertainers are recognizable by their stage wear alone. If you saw them out in anything other than what they wear while performing, you would hardly recognize them. Many musicians and actors could go in and out of character simply by changing shirts or hats. Others were the same, onstage or off.

Johnny Cash is one of those. The "Man in Black" they call him. I always wondered if there were any white clothes to do in that household's laundry. Did he wear black boxers? Even his hair was jet black. Johnny was tall, big, and to me, scary, although always polite. He smiled that crooked smile of his, but his deep voice made the floorboards rattle. I did like to watch him in action though. He would sling his guitar around and lean into the microphone when he sang. John was very much in love with his wife, June Carter Cash. They flirted with each other onstage and off. Always affectionate in public you could almost hear little birds tweeting above them when they were together. June sang with him on the *Opry* and sometimes she performed with her family. Her recent death was heartbreaking for everyone who knew them. Seeing John without her by his side is a very sad sight.

The Carter Family first started singing during the Depression. They were responsible for turning many unfamiliar songs into standards that everyone is familiar with today. During the folk music revival in the sixties, Mother Maybelle of the original Carter Family and her daughters June, Anita, and Helen became regulars on the *Grand Ole Opry* after having been named members in 1950. They were known as Mother Maybelle and the Carter Family. They carried with them the long legacy of being "Country Music's First Family."

We would sometimes visit Maybelle at her home. She was slight and gentle. I would play with Helen's youngest son, Kevin, when we were there. I always thought they were saying, "Cabin" so that's what I usually

Johnny Cash and his wife, June, backstage at the Opry House in 1975 waiting to go on the show. Behind them is Jerry Strobel, Opry manager at the time. "Baby" Ray of football fame is in the foreground, right. Dot Leverett is in the center of the photo looking right at Les. Libby is on the very far right. PHOTOGRAPH BY LES LEVERETT.

Waylon Jennings and Johnny Cash at the taping of one of Johnny's shows at the Ryman for ABC-TV in 1970. PHOTOGRAPH BY LES LEVERETT.

called him. Cabin came to play at our house a few times when we were very small, and it seemed that we were at their home a lot, since my brothers were close friends with his older brothers.

Daddy worked with Johnny and June quite often at the *Opry* and did the still photography for Johnny's syndicated television show. The *Johnny Cash Show* brought in many of the great actors, singers, musicians, and entertainers of our time. Louis Armstrong, Pete Seeger, Brenda Lee, Jose Feliciano, Arlo Guthrie, Bobby Gentry, The Everly Brothers, Dusty Springfield, Rod McKuen, Tammy Wynette, Neil Diamond, Jack Palance, Ray Charles, Jerry Lee Lewis, Jimmy Rodgers, Vicki Carr, Carl Perkins, O. C. Smith, Bob Hope, Mama Cass, Kenny Rogers and the First Edition, Burl Ives, Hank Williams Jr., Jeannie C. Riley, Merle Haggard, George Gobel, Waylon Jennings, Jackie DeShannon, Michael Parks, Gordon Terry, Roy Orbison, Shel Silverstein, Tony Joe White, Sonny James, Patti Page, Tex Ritter, Roy Acuff, Lynn Anderson, the Glaser Brothers, Charley Pride, Danny Davis and the Nashville Brass, Glen Campbell, Norman Blake, Red Lane, Bob Dylan, and The Statler Brothers were all on his show, as was a then-unknown Linda Ronstadt.

Ray Charles at the taping of one of Johnny's shows at the Ryman in 1970. PHOTOGRAPH BY LES LEVERETT.

I remember going with my daddy to those television tapings at the *Opry*. They were very long and drawn out, going on for many hours, taping the same scenes over and over. I

Sonny James at the taping of one of Johnny's shows at the Ryman in 1970.
PHOTOGRAPH BY LES LEVERETT.

Kenny Rogers at the taping of one of Johnny's shows at the Ryman in 1970.
PHOTOGRAPH BY LES LEVERETT.

loved it, but it was a great test of patience for me. It was also exciting seeing the lights, cameras, and all the people working hard to make a show
come together, but sometimes I felt captive at these shows. Since the
audience shots had to look the same for the whole show, no one could
really leave.

The same rules went for the *Bobby Lord Show*. Bobby once asked me
if I watched his show. I told him no, because it came on at the same time
as the *Mickey Mouse Club* show. He would carry on as if his feelings were
hurt. Of course, I never fell for it. I mean, everybody knows the big mouse
always wins.

Bobby Lord with Libby and unidentified children backstage at the Ryman in 1967.
PHOTOGRAPH BY LES LEVERETT.

Puppeteer Jim Henson sitting in the Ryman during rehearsals for *The Jimmy Dean Show* in 1964. PHOTOGRAPH BY LES LEVERETT.

Jim Henson working the muppet Rolf at W.S.M. *Studio C* during rehearsals for *The Jimmy Dean Show* in 1964. The Jordanaires (Ray Walker, Gordon Stoker, Hoyt Hawkins, and Neal Matthews) and Jimmy are also in this shot (Jimmy Dean is right behind Rolf.) PHOTOGRAPH BY LES LEVERETT.

Puppeteer Jim Henson was becoming a household name with his muppets when he came to the Ryman for the taping of *The Jimmy Dean Show.* I had looked forward to seeing Jim Henson for a week. When I finally met him, I was surprised that he didn't have my favorite character, Rolf, with him. Heck, that was why I wanted to see him. I noticed a large suitcase by his side, but it didn't occur to me that he would keep Rolf in there. Rolf, the big piano-playing, furry dog was always so alive to me. Daddy had to photograph him, so Jim took Rolf out of the case for me to "meet." I was appalled to the point of tears and had to turn away. I had no idea that Rolf was not real and that Jim put his arms into Rolf's to make them move and moved his mouth with sticks. It totally traumatized me. Mom knew never to bring that episode up.

Linda Ronstadt at the taping of one of Johnny's shows at the Ryman in 1970.
PHOTOGRAPH BY LES LEVERETT.

One Saturday night at the *Opry*, a few days after a taping of the *Johnny Cash Show*, I remember Mom and Estelle Akeman whispering and giggling about something that had nothing to do with me or Rolf. It was about the new singer, Linda Ronstadt, and how she was so pretty but somebody should tell her to wear a longer skirt. There were even rumors that she was not wearing underwear (oh my!) beneath that short skirt at the TV taping.

Her short skirt was a backstage topic for years. Stringbean didn't notice. He was so tall, her skirt looked just fine from where he stood. Daddy convinced Mom that he never noticed the skirt, but he did notice she was not wearing shoes.

Of course, Daddy *was* busy.

Daddy was involved with so many aspects of the entertainment industry. He was involved with the Western Film Collectors (WFC) for years. He did all their photography, and Mom and I would go along to the festivals and help staff the registration desks. I served as general gopher. Many of the festivals were held in Nashville, so we got to have a vacation in our own hometown. It was there that I met the likes of singing cowboys Ray Whitley, Eddie Dean, Johnny Bond, Rex Allen, James Warren, and Ray "Crash" Corrigan. Al Hoxie was one of my favorites. He served as my grandfather for the week of the festivals. He had been in silent movies, and I heard great tales of his adventures in film.

"Crash" wore a bolo tie with a squirrel's head clasp. It had little fake antlers to look like a tiny deer head. Invariably, when anyone would talk to him, his or her hand would end up reaching out to touch this odd bolo clasp. As soon as their hand got within inches of it, he would snort and scare the daylights out of that person.

Silver screen legend and *Opry* member, Tex Ritter, and his actress wife, Dorothy, were usually guests of honor at these festivals. One of their sons, Tom, sometimes helped Mom and me with registration by keeping us company. In between my duties, I would sneak off to view one of the many western movies that played around the clock at the festivals. It was

Ray Whitley and Ray "Crash" Corrigan at the Western Film Festival in Nashville in 1974. PHOTOGRAPH BY LES LEVERETT.

great to see these actors singing on the silver screen in their youth. It put it all into perspective for me. From growing up backstage at the Ryman, I had a good idea of what a live radio show was like. I knew what it was like to see an hour-long television show being taped. When I would watch these sometimes hilarious western films, I was aware of what went into the making of such a film. I knew it was a lot, especially in the days of the silent films, so I was in awe of these great actors. I knew that in their prime, a day of filming for them meant a *full* day of filming without many comforts.

Publicity events for the festival were lined up for the guests of honor long before their arrival in Nashville. One busy day, Daddy had to stay at the festival to photograph an event. He asked if I would accompany a couple of the actors to their TV interview and do the photography for him. I wasn't driving yet, so Mom became the chauffeur. Off we went, with Crash Corrigan in his cowboy duds and Iron Eyes Cody in full Indian garb to Channel 4 studios in Nashville. I felt honored to have the responsibility of photographing a job for my daddy. We got several stares on the highway, but they did not compare to the ones we received in a restaurant when we stopped for lunch. I was about fifteen, so I was not fond of the stares and, not believing my fortune that day, spent it laughing nervously. Nonetheless, I enjoyed my time with these characters. That day Crash taught me the merits of eating parsley: clear skin and fresh breath. There I was in a crowded restaurant with my mom, a cowboy, and an Indian, eating the garnish off everyone's plate.

Since I had grown up at the *Opry*, I volunteered to go with Ray Whitley when he performed on the *Grand Ole Opry* during the WFC.

Eddie Dean, Ray Whitley, and Dorothy Ritter being interviewed by Ralph Emery in Nashville in 1974. PHOTOGRAPH BY LES LEVERETT.

Someone drove us to the Opry House from the hotel, and I remember Ray holding my hand like a sweet grandfather. He sang all the way there. When his time came to go out on the stage, he walked out without a nerve in his body, sang a smooth cowboy song, and it seemed like he had been there every Saturday night of his life.

(l to r) Iron Eyes Cody, Wayne Rogers, Monty Montana, Tex Williams, Libby, and George Montgomery at the Acuff Theater at Opryland in 1981. PHOTOGRAPH BY LES LEVERETT.

Back at the festival, Ray Whitley performed his famous rope act for the evening's entertainment. He needed two assistants, so he asked Doug Green, of Riders in the Sky, and me. I had to hold a thickly rolled-up piece of newspaper for him to whip out of my hand with his bullwhip. He did the same with Doug, except Doug had to hold the paper between his teeth. Ray joked that if he was going to miss and mess up someone's face, he would rather it be Doug's. Me, too! It was tense, and I recall closing my eyes after I stuck my arm out to the side. I was so nervous I had to hold my arm with my other hand to keep it steady. I opened my eyes once I heard the loud crack of the bullwhip and roar of applause. My hand was still intact. Our segment was followed by Ray's wonderful act of jumping in and out of his twirling rope. There is definitely an art to a rope act.

Ray Whitley and Libby performing a rope act at the film festival in 1974.
PHOTOGRAPH BY LES LEVERETT.

Before the show, while Ray was explaining to Doug and me what was going to take place, he was twirling his rope around and talking at the same time. Doug was really paying attention. I noticed Ray show him a few extra pointers. Doug is now a pretty darn good roper. He let me hold the rope and I was shocked at just how heavy it was. I don't know how it ever leaves the ground.

When Riders in the Sky first came on the scene, they hung out at the *Grand Ole Opry* all the time. Too Slim, Woody Paul, and Doug were onto something good and unique, and it was great that someone noticed. They were keeping the world of western music alive and giving us something fresh, new, and colorful. It was actually something old and familiar, just forgotten for a while. Daddy and I once collaborated on an album cover for The Riders in the Sky. He took the photograph, and I handcolored it. The goal was to make it look like an old western lobby card complete with gaudy colors. Chaps, fringe, cow patterns, ten-gallon hats, and even their gait set The Riders in the Sky apart. I noticed that western entertainers don't come out of character, as far as their stage clothes go, as often as the country entertainers do. You could run into Doug, Woody Paul, or Too Slim out at the grocery, and I guarantee you they would at least have on cowboy boots or a giant belt buckle.

It was a good thing Stringbean didn't wear his stage clothes anywhere but for shows. When I was little, I always felt anxious and shy around

The Riders in the Sky on the *Opry*. PHOTOGRAPH BY LIBBY LEVERETT-CREW.

Stringbean because I feared that his low riding pants would fall off right in front of me.

Daddy said the first time he photographed String, he had come up to his studio in his stage outfit. The first thing String said was, "You like to go fishin' boy? We'll go sometime." What a magnificent thank-you from someone who felt a fishing trip was worth a bag of gold.

Stringbean performing with (l to r) Larry McNeely, Jackie Phelps, Jimmy Riddle, Roy Acuff, Harold Weakley, Tommy Jackson, and Lester Wilburn at the Ryman in 1967. PHOTOGRAPH BY LES LEVERETT.

One year, the *Opry* people decided that the next *Opry* pictorial history book should have photographs of the members showing off their favorite hobby. One day, Daddy took two portraits at a lake with String and Billy Grammer, both avid fishermen. He says that in all the years he knew String, they never got to go fishing together. But the invitation was a nice thought.

Stringbean's friends just called him String. He was a close friend of Grandpa Jones, and Daddy loved to be in their company as they played off each other's humor and laughed together. They were such good friends that they even shared a property line. They also appeared together for years on *Hee Haw*, a syndicated television show taped in Nashville.

(clockwise) Grandpa Jones, Merle Travis, Junior Samples, Lulu Roman, Roy Acuff, Archie Campbell, and George "Goober" Lindsay on the *Hee Haw* set in 1982. PHOTOGRAPH BY LES LEVERETT.

Hee Haw was an unexpected success. It originally aired as a summer replacement for *The Smothers Brothers' Comedy Hour* in 1969. No one, except maybe the original writers, expected it to last twenty-eight years. The show was an hour of cornball humor and entertainment, and for the first time, being a country hick was okay. As an adult, I was hired to photograph a few *Hee Haw* tapings. I knew everyone on the set, including the stagehands, so it was a very comfortable gig. Everything was always kept light at these tapings. After all, everyone was having fun, laughing, doing what he or she liked to do best, and being paid very well for it.

I once went to a *Hee Haw* cast party at the home of the costume designer for the show. It was funny how everyone was the same. Pranks and laughter were all around. Junior Samples was still in his overalls. It just felt like a family reunion instead of a cast party. The only things missing were the TV cameras, the cornfield, and String.

Stringbean was not at the *Hee Haw* cast party that night, and his humor was greatly missed. He and his wife, Estelle, had been murdered years before. That loss and the way it occurred were not talked about much in our circles. It was just too painful. The only thing talked about was how everyone should keep his or her money in the bank. It was common knowledge that String disliked and did not trust banking establishments and chose to keep his money in the bib pocket of his overalls and in jars around his tiny home.

One Saturday night, we were all at the Ryman together. Everyone was laughing and happy. My mother and Estelle were sharing a box of popcorn (and probably still talking about Linda Ronstadt's skirt). String performed. Daddy chatted with him. They came in the same way; they went home the same way. The next morning, we heard the horrible news that String and Estelle were dead. It was such a shock. How could someone I had just seen hours before be gone forever? How could two very kind, simple, gentle people have their lives snuffed out?

Every time an entertainer died, Daddy had to immediately go into the darkroom to print photos for the media. I always thought that it must have been especially hard on him, until I had my own darkroom. Now I know that it was a comfort to be left alone, quiet and literally in the dark, watching images of loved ones come up in the developing tray, letting the tears drip in. It was a part of the grieving process. My daddy experienced it many times over, and now, I understand.

Daddy printed many photos of String for the press. Of course, he enjoyed it when String was alive and the prints were going out to further his career. But from the time String died, those prints became historic. Daddy could not go back and reshoot or get a more current image. He would no longer wait in his studio for String to put on that ridiculous outfit. He and String would not talk about going fishing one day.

String and Estelle left behind no children, but they had touched the lives of many with their gentle ways. String had sent many a banjo tune and a lot of laughter out into the cosmos. This was their contribution, maybe simple, but quite grand.

CHANGES THE SIZE
OF TEXAS

When it was time for the Girl Scouts and Brownies to sell cookies, I was a shoo-in for the "One Hundred Cookies Sold" pin.

All I had to do was don my Brownie uniform, complete with brown beanie hat, pack my little cardboard boxes of Thin Mints, Peanut Butter Patty, and Shortbread cookies and carry along my collection envelope to the Ryman with Daddy.

It seemed that I didn't have to do anything but smile and collect money. Everyone came to me. I could hardly make it from Mr. Bell's spot by the backstage door to the little café tables, where I liked to perch, for the people stopping me wanting to buy cookies. My supplies were depleted by the time I was ready to get serious about that golden pin I knew I was going to "earn."

One of my best customers was a man named Tex Ritter. His name sounded as big and strong as his frame and his home state of Texas. He hailed from Murvall, in Panola County.

Tex came to Nashville in the mid-sixties by way of Hollywood and brought his wife and leading lady, Dorothy Fay. After a very successful career in the movies, he became a member of the *Grand Ole Opry* and worked for WSM Radio. In 1970, he ran for one of Tennessee's U.S. senate seats. Daddy met Tex when he took his first publicity shot after he and Dorothy moved to Nashville.

As a little girl, I always thought Tex resembled Santa Claus. His belly entered the room before he did. With the exception of the white hair and beard, he had the act down, right to the pipe that he kept going in one hand, and the squinty eyes. His loud, "Hee, Hee" could

Tex and Dorothy Fay on the set of *Sundown on the Prairie* in 1939. FROM THE
COLLECTION OF LES LEVERETT.

almost pass for a jolly "Ho, Ho". His nose was round and bulbous and
his bottom lip was pouty. He towered over me, and even over many
adults.

Backstage at the *Opry*, he always had on his western duds. He wore
beautiful cowboy boots in nice colors with fancy stitching and usually a
suit trimmed with white or red piping around the western cut. It was
stitched with the same color thread over the little arrow designs coming
down from the pockets. A string tie or a large bolo tie was the final touch,
and that was what I suppose classified him as western and not country.

He always moved slow and turned his head and shoulders at the
same time as if the vertebra in his neck were fused together, sort of like
Ed Sullivan. When he walked up that backstage hall to go out for his

TEX RITTER

Tex Ritter autographed this 1967 photograph for Libby. FROM THE COLLECTION OF LES LEVERETT.

performance, those old wood floor planks would squeak. When he talked, he had a great voice that boomed and pronunciations I have never heard since. Dorothy was "Dawthe".

When Tex signed his name, he always drew this little symbol at the end of his last name. I asked him about it once, and after he explained it was a way to say *friend* in Spanish, he showed me how to draw this symbol. I spent hours trying to perfect that symbol and work it into my signature.

Many of the songs he did were what I call "story songs" or ballads. "Froggy Went a Courtin'," "Hillbilly Heaven," "Boll Weevil," "Jingle Jangle Jingle," and "Big Rock Candy Mountain" were some of his big hits. He had such a unique style, strumming his guitar, which was dwarfed against his large body. His voice was so deep it rattled the rafters. (My dad does a perfect imitation of him, by the way.) He was a real singing cowboy and a giant in more ways than one.

Daddy thought the world of him. And if Daddy thought a lot of someone, I knew that they were good, because Daddy was a good man. There were tales of how Tex would help his band members and others with anything he could. He would hand out money, bail musicians out of jail, or do whatever was needed. He helped children in need. He was just a big guy with a big heart the size of Texas or maybe just the size of Santa Claus.

Dorothy Fay missed a good chance at being Mrs. Claus. She was bubbly and flitted around the place in maternal overdrive making sure everyone was taken care of and had what they needed. A "Dear" preceded everything she said. She seemed to be about two feet off the ground and rarely sat down. When she did sit, she looked like she would fall over in a deep sleep. She was one of those ladies who could do high heels and did indeed wear them most of the time, but any chance she had she took them off. I remember seeing her pad around in her stocking feet at odd places or times. She always wore nice dresses with a scarf around her neck. I never saw her in pants; maybe because her legs were so great, she knew they shouldn't be hidden. When she smiled, her whole face smiled, and she had a look, as though she had a question, or was surprised. Maybe it was a Hollywood thing. Maybe it was just Dorothy.

Dorothy, Tex, John, and Tom Ritter taken in 1951 when they lived in Van Nuys, California. FROM THE COLLECTION OF LES LEVERETT.

The Ritter family (Tex, John, Tommy, and Dorothy) at their Nashville home in 1971. PHOTOGRAPH BY LES LEVERETT.

She used to say that by sleeping with her feet higher than her head, she could get four hours of sleep a night and it was equivalent to getting eight. I wondered if she slept in those high heels.

Always smiling that Hollywood smile and animated as she could be, Dorothy had a way of making everyone feel like they were her best friends. The mother of two sons, John and Tom, I always felt like she liked me simply because of my gender. She enjoyed the presence of a little girl in pigtails and ribbons, I suppose. Actually, she seemed to like all kids. Several of us second-generation "*Opry* fixtures" sometimes called her Aunt Dorothy.

At Christmas, the florist always delivered a live poinsettia to our house. Mom probably always had a good idea who had sent it, but she would let me open the tiny envelope to read the card. Dorothy always personally signed it in huge swirly letters.

Not long after the poinsettia arrived, we would get a special delivery package from Tiffany and Co. of New York. It was usually a large box with small, individual gift boxes inside. The Tiffany boxes are a lovely shade of robin's egg blue with silver ribbons. I loved those fine gifts the Ritters used to send, all of which I will always treasure. There was a magnificent sterling silver pen in its own little Tiffany and Co. blue pouch, a monogrammed muffler, a silver bookmark shaped like a heart with "Libby" engraved on it, and my favorite, a lovely Victorian-style angel who held a candle. The tiny little candle had a tiny little bulb that lit up.

When it came to giving gifts to the Ritters, my mom was always at a loss. They had everything, so she did what she did best during the holidays: she made candy. Mom didn't just make fudge. She made penuche and divinity, coconut bonbons, peanut butter balls, chocolate-covered cherries, chocolate-covered pretzels, and rum balls that made the whole house smell like a party. I helped her with our holiday custom. Sometimes we would slip in a prank by covering a chunk of cheese in chocolate just so we could see the disgusted look on my brothers' faces when one of them decided to sample the candy without permission. We made candy for a good day and into the night and spent another day packaging our goods into cute little assortments to deliver.

When we took the Ritters their box of candy, Dorothy acted like it was a priceless treasure and immediately began sampling our handiwork. Her whole face would smile.

The Ritters lived in Nashville at the corner of Franklin Road and Curtiswood Lane right up from Minnie Pearl and the governor. Theirs was a sprawling ranch house, and I mean sprawling. When we would visit, a maid always answered the door, with Dorothy right behind her, then Tex. I never got the feeling that their maid was a servant, more like she was a friend who just helped around the house. Dad said that when Tex made out his last will and testament, he had her serve as a witness.

When we would visit, Mom and Dad would settle into the living room by the fireplace right off the foyer. Dad would eventually go off to another part of the house to visit with Tex, and I would play with a couple of the many cats that also lived there. Sooner or later, I would wander off. It was a great place to explore. One room led to another, which led to another, and so on, until I had a difficult time finding my way back to the adults. Although their home was spacious, it was very cluttered. Just plain cluttered with stuff sitting around all stacked up. There were boxes that looked like their contents had not seen daylight since they left California years before. Magazines, newspapers, stacks of shoes, movie memorabilia, you name it, it was stacked in that house. They had a great, lovely, long dining table (at least as a child, it seemed long and elegant to me) where we shared a few meals with the Ritters.

One of Tex's favorite meals was chipped beef on toast. We had dinner one night with them, and I expected the maid to be doing the cooking, but instead, there came Dorothy running in and out of the kitchen, through what I thought was really cool—a butler door, which could go either way. With Dorothy going in and out of it, it looked like a revolving door. She brought drinks, made toast, brought out more chipped beef, handed over the recipe to my mom, then brought more drinks. She almost made us dizzy. Tex would rear back in his chair and watch her for a while, with a quiet little, "Hee, Hee" slipping out and those squinty eyes smiling. He got a chuckle out of his leading lady.

On the other hand, she, in a fun-loving way, drove him crazy. He would complain that every time he went out of town he would come back to something new and that Dorothy had spent more of his money. Once, he came home to find the sewing room converted into an extra bathroom. He complained and complained until the first time he had to use the facility. Then he noticed that the design was of naked ladies. Dorothy had not really noticed what exactly made the different shades of dark and light on her new wallpaper, she just liked the color. He came out and in that big voice announced, "I spent thirty minutes in your new bathroom and I feel thirty years younger!"

Tex never really cared what people thought. He was a confident guy and didn't hold back on his feelings or thoughts. One time backstage at the *Opry* he came thundering into the room saying, "Who the hell has this ugly Cadillac parked out back with lips painted all over it?" A very timid Ernie Ashworth walked up in his rhinestone suit and said proudly, but like a shy schoolboy, "Me, Mr. Ritter." Tex gave him a good looking over and realized that his rhinestone design was of giant red lips all over the yellow suit, then huffed, "Figures." (Ernie Ashworth's big hit was "Talk Back Trembling Lips" and from the moment it hit the charts, his theme was giant red lips.) The funny thing was, no one ever seemed to get his or her feelings hurt by Tex. He was just an open person, and he usually spoke the truth, so every one accepted this as just Tex being Tex.

As a child, I was always shy around Tex. I don't know if it was his loudness, or his size, but I always felt in awe of him, and speechless. I remember sitting on his knee one time backstage, his big polar bear hand holding me safe around my middle. He sang "Get Along Little Dogies." I could hardly look at him I was so bashful.

(l to r) Willie Nelson, D.J. Jim Kizzia, an unidentified D.J., Ernie Ashworth (in his "lip suit"), another unidentified D.J., and Les Leverett backstage at the Ryman in 1965. FROM THE COLLECTION OF LES LEVERETT.

Backstage at the Ryman, Dad would sometimes leave me in Tex's care if he had to go out front at the last minute, or if it was raining. (He would go get the car and pull up to the back door, hop out, and come get me.) Tex would ask about what I had been doing and what I liked to do. He would hum a song or two looking for ways to entertain me. We'd discuss Girl Scout Cookies, salamanders, and my drawings. All the while, he would be puffing on that pipe of his. When Dad would fetch me, Tex would give me a funny order, like, "You watch out for that crazy daddy of yours!" He would laugh that "hee, hee" laugh of his and Dad would give him some grief. They always parted laughing and with a good strong handshake, and sometimes a half hug. You know, the kind that men do.

Tex and Dorothy's son Tom was backstage almost as much as I was. He sometimes shared a café table with me in the open mailroom. He was a great combination of what made us all love his parents. He was strong and kind, always smiling, and loved to laugh. Tom had cerebral palsy and sometimes when I was older, we would share our feelings of how sometimes we felt different from other people. He felt different because of his physical challenges, me, because of my creative, abstract way of looking at life. Tom always liked my parents and spent many an hour chatting with my mom. Mom could make anyone feel comfortable with her conversation.

John Ritter, Libby Leverett, and Tom Ritter backstage at the Ryman in 1973. PHOTOGRAPH BY LES LEVERETT.

I was in serious puppy love with both of those Ritter boys. I had admired them my whole childhood, but the older I got, the crazier I felt about them. John once gave me an autographed photo. It said, "To my secret sweetheart, Love, John Ritter." It was my prized possession, and the last thing I looked at before I fell asleep at night for at least six months. I wrote John really silly love notes that I mailed to his Hollywood office. (To this day, my face reddens to think of it.) I suddenly became tongue-tied when I sat with Tom backstage.

Tom ran for delegate to the Tennessee Constitutional Convention one year, and he and Dorothy asked if I would help campaign. Boy, was I ever thrilled with such an honor. Kelly, one of my girlfriends, rode the school bus home with me from Goodlettsville High School on election day. We got dressed up, and Mom took us out to the Ritters' to pick up all of the material and have a briefing with Dorothy. She opened that garage door, where all of the signs and pamphlets had been stored, and I remember thinking how there was not room for one more, thin piece of paper in that place. Like the house, it was stacked to the top and bulging. Our instructions were to stand outside the polls at a local elementary school and talk Tom up. It was no problem for me; I thought he hung the moon. We had said his name so many times and had talked so much, we were hoarse by the time Mom came back for us later that night.

It took me a good year or two to get over my crush on those Ritter boys. Reality hit the day I realized that they were about ten years older than me (ancient!) and not in the least bit interested in me. It didn't hurt that I had begun to notice boys that were my own age for a change.

Tom's younger brother, John, was following in his parents' footsteps and had never fully moved to Tennessee with the family. He stayed in California and worked on his career. His first major break came when he was cast in the pilot for *The Waltons* television series. He played the Reverend Fordwick. After filming, he came to Nashville for one of his many visits. We were invited over for drinks, dinner, to meet his latest "leading lady," and a viewing of the show, which he had brought with

(clockwise) John Ritter, Tom Ritter, Ginger Smith, Libby Leverett, John's friend, Jo Walker, and Jo's daughter Michelle, and Dorothy Ritter in the Ritter home in 1975. PHOTOGRAPH BY LES LEVERETT.

him on a big sixteen-millimeter reel. We sat around that front living room of theirs, I was on the floor, and we watched and cheered when he came into view. He told us some of the inside stories of the filming, and the whole room was full of excitement. Most of us forgot that the reason we were together that night was to help Dorothy, Tom, and John through the first anniversary of Tex's death.

Tex had died in January of 1974. Tom was with him and was devastated. That was the saddest I had seen my daddy. He was angry, sad, and quiet. Although I was a teenager, I didn't understand. I couldn't think of Tex not being around. At the funeral home, I watched John and Tom, surrounded by crying people and I wondered how they felt. I could not let myself think of such a thing as losing my own father. I watched Daddy going from friend to friend, hug to handshake. It was really hard on him.

I was in my sophomore year in high school when Tom graduated from Vanderbilt's School of Law. My mom surprised me by picking me up early at school that spring day so I could go home to get ready for the graduation ceremony. I had a new dress for the occasion. Mom and I picked up Daddy then met Dorothy on campus. She was "busting her buttons" she was so proud. The early spring sun was strong, and she had her parasol with her to keep the sun off her light skin. She also had tears in her eyes as did my mom and I, and I think I saw the sun glimmer a little on Daddy's cheeks, too. We were all so very proud of Tom. I know that Tex was somewhere smiling.

After the graduation, we went on to their church for a reception, then to the house of some of the Ritters' close friends for a special dinner in Tom's honor. I remember feeling so grown-up. I was the youngest one

Tom Ritter's graduation from Vanderbilt. FROM THE COLLECTION OF LES LEVERETT.

Tex Ritter backstage at the Ryman in 1973, a few months before he died. This is Libby's favorite photo that Les took of Tex. PHOTOGRAPH BY LES LEVERETT.

there and I was actually included in the conversation as an adult. It didn't do much for my nerves that night, but I loved feeling I was part of everything around me.

In March 1974, the *Grand Ole Opry* moved to its new home at Opryland, which was a musical theme park east of downtown Nashville on the Cumberland River. Tex never got to play on that stage.

The Ryman remained closed for many years. I missed the smells of old, worn wood and the creaky floors. I missed the stained glass windows and the sweaty, happy crowds.

The new Opry House was state-of-the-art. Everyone had his or her own dressing room. There was a lounge. A television studio was in the back. It was all so very different. What remained the same were the people. I learned at a young age that this was what mattered most. James was still running around sweating as he ran errands and moved things. Rosa still lined up the lemonade. The guard was still at the back door. The popcorn was still out front. My dad was still all over the place taking photos. My mom was still sitting around talking with the ladies. The taps still clicked, the dresses twirled, and the rhinestones glimmered. The fans still came from all over the world. They still clapped. (But, they didn't fan themselves as much in the air-conditioned facility.) And the music played. If you closed your eyes you could still hear the deep, bold, "Hee, Hee" of Tex Ritter.

Years later, John took his baby son, Jason, to visit the Opry. He took him out on the stage, and he held him on the big circle of stage floor they had cut and moved from the original Ryman stage for the new Opry House stage. Jason's fresh eyes squinted under the bright lights. I could have sworn I saw Tex.

Not long after the *Opry* moved, Dorothy began working there as a sort of goodwill ambassador. When a celebrity would come to the *Opry*, it was her job to show them around, entertain them, and give them boxes of GooGoos that were given out as publicity by the Standard Candy Company, a sponsor of the *Grand Ole Opry*. Part of Dad's job was

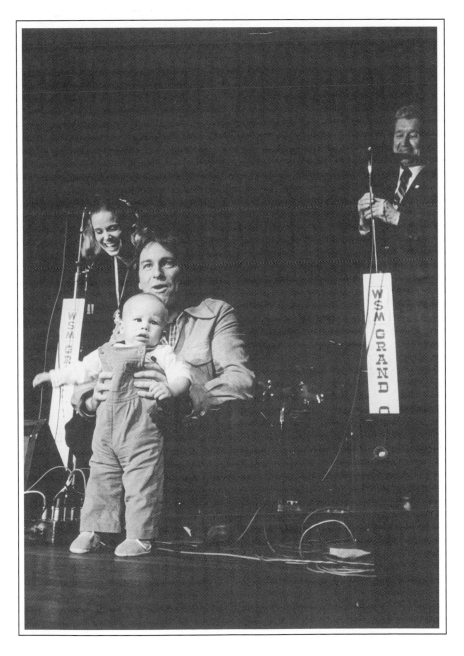

John Ritter holding his son Jason on the stage of the Opry House in 1980. Nancy Morgan, Jason's mother, is on the left. Roy Acuff is in the background. PHOTOGRAPH BY LES LEVERETT.

Libby (holding Dorothy Ritter's shoes under her coat) with Jamie Wyeth at Opryland in 1977. PHOTOGRAPH BY LES LEVERETT.

to go along with Dorothy as she entertained these celebrities so he could photograph the adventure. (A delicious fringe benefit: a couple of boxes of those wonderful chocolatey GooGoos. They indirectly helped the sales of the company that made Clearasil.)

Dad always knew that I loved to be with him, and I was old enough at that time to really help him with his equipment.

One night we arrived at the Opry House to discover that we were to tag along with Dorothy and famous American artists Andy Warhol and Jamie Wyeth. My Dad had started letting me help him take photographs with his cameras. He knew that I had a growing love for the visual arts and that this was the best way to teach me. I had spent my early childhood years watching, now it was time for me to have hands-on experience. That night, he gently put the strap of a newly loaded camera around my neck, and as he held my hair up and straightened it up, he said, "Why don't you shoot a few tonight?" I felt like he had placed an Olympic gold medal around my neck.

We took Andy Warhol and Jamie Wyeth all around the Opry House, backstage and out front, and then to the plaza area outside. It was a funny little assemblage of people. Because we were doing a lot of walking, Dorothy took off her high heels. She stuffed them in a grocery bag and guess who got to carry them? I honestly didn't mind. I was in heaven. There I was, helping my dad take pictures, helping Dorothy, and hanging out with two of my most admired artists.

Warhol didn't have much to say, but we did connect that evening when I took a head-on shot of him sitting on the risers on the *Opry* stage. Jamie Wyeth, on the other hand was talkative and very down to earth. I just about died when he asked if we'd send him some photos, and he jotted their home address in Pennsylvania down on a piece of paper and gave it to Dad. For a split second, I envisioned myself tracking him down in his studio to check out his art supplies and his new paintings, maybe even meet the rest of the Wyeth clan. This never happened, of course, but we did send him the photos he had requested and asked him to sign and return one to me for my collection. He graciously obliged.

Daddy was a great art and art history buff, and Mom actually went to Ringling Brothers School of Art in Sarasota, Florida. I had been around good art all my life and had taken many classes, even as a child. Dad was as excited as I was about working with these guys. He had always been a big fan of the entire artistic Wyeth family. We kept elbowing each other and shooting knowing glances to each other throughout that magical night. It was wonderful to share such a once-in-a-lifetime evening with Daddy.

When I went to school the next Monday and told all my friends about how I got to not only meet, but also hang out for hours with Warhol and Wyeth, not a single one of them knew who the heck I was talking about. It wasn't until I was grown and worked with other artists, that my night with these people was appreciated.

Andy Warhol sitting on the *Opry* stage in 1977. PHOTOGRAPH BY LIBBY LEVERETT-CREW

I continued to go to work at the *Grand Ole Opry* with my dad and in my teenage years shot my first professional photographic job there. An album cover was soon to follow. I was hooked. Music and photography were in my blood. Really.

Tom Ritter, Libby Leverett-Crew, Allison Crew, and John Ritter sitting on the stage at the Opry House in 1997. PHOTOGRAPH BY LARRY HILL.

Dad half-jokingly told me never to marry a musician or go into photography. Oh well. Years later, while at John Hartford's house one cold winter night I found myself surrounded by the people of my childhood. As the music played and the Cumberland River rolled by, I met the man who is now my husband. Yes, he is a musician. I don't have to tell you what career I chose. Maybe I should mention that our young daughter dreams of being a singer.

My daughter has now stood on the sidelines backstage at the Opry House. The third generation is coming along. No doubt, Daddy, Tex, and other various stars that shone on those Saturday nights had an influence.

IN THE CIRCLE OF
FAMILY AND FRIENDS

My mother called me in to the television set with a shriek of surprise and laughter. There, on the local six o'clock news was my daddy, in the fountain in front of the Hall of Fame with none other than Dolly Parton. His pants were rolled up to his knees, his camera was dangling from his neck, and he was helping Dolly dip her toe in. He was photographing her for an album cover.

Les Leverett in the fountain at the old Country Music Hall of Fame in Nashville with Dolly Parton. FROM THE COLLECTION OF LES LEVERETT.

He was ribbed about this for months. He took it with a grin and a grain of salt and went about his business. He and Dolly went way back, and it didn't bother him one bit. Besides, the album cover for *Bubbling Over* looked great and won the Country Album Cover of the year from *Billboard* in 1973.

Pearl Butler, Johnny Cash, and Carl Butler backstage at the Ryman in 1962. PHOTOGRAPH BY LES LEVERETT.

The first time Daddy met Dolly, she was hanging around the Friday night *Opry*. At that time, the show was called *The Friday Night Frolics*. He was backstage talking with Carl and Pearl Butler, who were up-and-coming songwriters and entertainers. Dolly was young, and at that time the general public in Nashville had not heard much about her. When she saw the Butlers, she ran, like a child, to hug and greet them. Carl and Pearl were friends of Dolly's. They had all seen very lean days in East Tennessee and knew the importance of a good friendship and a good song.

Carl and Pearl lived in the Hillsboro Village area of Nashville in a warm, cozy house with an old player piano that had its player removed. With Pearl's crazy humor, good cooking, and that piano, their home drew in other musicians trying to find their way in the business. Marty Robbins used to drop in for a meal and would play into the night, singing for everyone who happened to be there. Dolly lived with Carl and Pearl when she first moved to Nashville.

The first annual Dolly Parton Day. (l to r) Pete Drake, Dave Kirby, D. J. Fontana (Elvis Presley's drummer), Dolly, and Bobby Dyson, in Sevierville, Tennessee, in 1970. PHOTOGRAPH BY LES LEVERETT.

I cannot imagine a more joyful person to have as a houseguest. Dolly was just Dolly and still is. Born and raised in very difficult times in Locust Ridge, in Sevier County, Tennessee, she had a heart of gold, a very positive outlook, and talent beyond words. Her wit was quick and of course, everyone loved her beauty. Her voice was sweet, and her career in Nashville blossomed and took her to other places.

No matter where her career took her in the early days, she would go back home to Sevier County to hold benefits at the local high school. My parents went on a couple of these trips to the mountains for Daddy to cover the events. While there, he actually shot two different album covers. Entertainers like Porter Wagoner, Stringbean, and the Blackwood Brothers joined Dolly at these benefits.

Dolly Parton, her father, and sister Stella in the parade in Sevierville. The man to the right, next to the car, is Cas Walker, who sponsored country singers to promote his grocery business and had been helping Dolly since she was nine. PHOTOGRAPH BY LES LEVERETT.

To this day she gives back. With her *Imagination Library* she makes sure that every child in her hometown (and now other counties and states) has a collection of books. She has helped the cause of literacy far more than she takes credit for.

Carl Butler signing autographs from the Ryman stage between shows in 1964. PHOTOGRAPH BY LES LEVERETT.

Daddy photographed Dolly in her early days on the *Grand Ole Opry*. He had a way of knowing when someone was going to make it and continue on the uphill track to stardom. When he heard Dolly, he knew she had what it took. He felt the same about Carl Butler. Daddy had been asked to photograph Carl in the studio. He said Carl was very expressive and moved a lot. After the shoot, he remarked to the coordinator that he had just photographed "country music's Elvis." The coordinator shook her head and said, "No, Les, he's just another singer wanting to make it big." Well, Daddy was right. Carl and Pearl had a top hit with a song called, "Don't Let Me Cross Over." He also wrote a song called, "If Teardrops Were Pennies." It was a hit for Carl Smith and Rosemary Clooney. It put the Butlers on the songwriting and performing map and helped them purchase a small ranch in Franklin, Tennessee, south of Nashville.

Carl at Crossover Acres in Franklin, Tennessee, in 1964. PHOTOGRAPH BY LES LEVERETT.

Like their home in the Village, "Crossover Acres," as they named their ranch, was a magnet for creative types. I loved our many visits to the country to roam on the farm, explore the vegetable garden, and ride the pony they had given me.

"Dynamite" was his name. It felt good to tell people that I had a pony, even though it really wasn't mine. I'm sure "Capearl," as I sometimes called Carl and Pearl, knew this.

Libby (on horse) at Crossover Acres with friends and family in 1967. PHOTOGRAPH BY LES LEVERETT.

There was a trick horse in the same enclosure as Dynamite. He was trained to go opposite of all directions he was given. Carl didn't tell this to Daddy. So, the first time he rode him, Daddy dug his heels in to get the horse to go and the horse dug his hooves in to keep from going. Frustrated, Daddy pulled on the reins and that horse took off like greased lightning. Every time he pulled on the reins to make it stop or yelled, "Whoa!" it ran faster. When he would pull right, the horse would go left, and so on. I remember everyone standing around the outside of the fence laughing their heads off watching Daddy being taken all over the meadow by the horse. Carl was laughing so hard he was bent over double and crying. He could hardly get the words out to tell Daddy what the problem was and how to remedy it.

It was always good to see Carl laugh. Like so many deep, creative thinkers, he was moody, sometimes depressed, and withdrawn. He and

Libby with Jake Tullock backstage at the Ryman in 1965. PHOTOGRAPH BY LES LEVERETT.

Daddy became close friends over the years, and it always worried Daddy when Carl was sullen and kept to himself. But, when he was up, he was up. He sat in the den singing and playing his guitar while carrying on conversation.

It seemed that every time we went to the Butlers, we were not alone. There were always other friends visiting. Marty Robbins still knew his way to the meals and the piano. Dolly showed up every now and then. Singers such as Roy Bee, Don Sauter, and Don Unterfer would be hanging around. "Cousin Jake" Tullock (who played with Flatt & Scruggs) was there so often for so many years I thought he just lived with the Butlers. Sometimes, I even had a playmate. Sally Smathers, my favorite, was a couple of years younger than me, and like myself had been born into this very interesting backstage view of music business life without having a musical person in her family. "The Stoney Mountain Cloggers" consisted of her parents and all of her siblings who danced on the Grand Ole Opry. We were used to seeing each other backstage. When at Carl's and Pearl's, we would spend hours chasing wild cats all over the ranch and played magnificent games of hide-and-seek.

When mealtime came around, we would sit down to grand southern dinners Pearl and Carl's mother, Mrs. Butler, would cook. There were bowls upon bowls of southern delights. Mounds of mashed potatoes, thick slices of ham, a large roast beef, gravy, fresh-grown creamed corn, tomatoes, and the only thing I could not eat . . . crackling cornbread. It was made with what Daddy calls "pig parts." It was way too chewy and mysterious for my taste, yet some consider it a southern delicacy.

At that time, my brothers had not been hanging out at the Ryman as much as they used to, but they liked to go with the family to visit Carl and Pearl. They could ride horses and fish in the pond with Daddy and Carl, and there were acres and acres of land to get lost on.

When I was little, and we would take those trips to the Butlers, I felt adored. Back then, Carl and Pearl had no children and they loved me so much. I always came home with gifts, clothes, and candy. When they toured, they would always bring me wonderful souvenirs. I always felt special in their company. As I look back, I realize there was a time when *my* family was having a lean period. Carl and Pearl came by our home and left boxes of groceries and gifts on our back porch. I heard them and when I peeked out the curtains, they motioned me to be quiet. I waited until their Cadillac had pulled out of the driveway before I told my parents.

In the same manner, for my third birthday, Carl snuck a swing set into our backyard and drove off. When I was older, they heard that I was interested in taking piano lessons and they knew we didn't have a piano. They had their old player piano moved to our home. It was put to good use during my older childhood, but during my teenage years grew a bit dusty in between having *Color My World* and *Cherish* picked out on the keys. When I married and moved out, it went with me, along with the blessings of Dolly Parton's sweet voice and Marty Robbins' nimble fingers.

Carl and Pearl Butler had a good run in the music business. They wrote some great songs that are still with us today. However, somewhere along the way, hard times came along again. By then, Dolly was doing well, and Dolly has never forgotten from where she came. In the music industry it is said she would send the Butlers a large check every Christmas to help them get through their difficult times.

For years, Dolly did the *Grand Ole Opry* and *The Porter Wagoner Show* with her singing partner, Porter Wagoner. They won awards for their duets and recorded several albums together. Daddy did the photography for their covers, sometimes using props from our home. On Dolly's album, *Burning the Midnight Oil*, she is looking into her hands at what the viewer knows is a photograph, although the image is not visible. It was a billfold-size photo of me Daddy had pulled from his wallet. On other covers our linens, our picture frames, our tables, even my family appear. And always, there were rhinestones. Rhinestones and studio lighting, they just sparkle.

Dolly on the set of *The Porter Wagoner Show* in Nashville in 1971. PHOTOGRAPH BY
LES LEVERETT.

When I think about all of the rhinestones I saw growing up in the
music industry, Porter's come to mind first. He was always a shine above
the rest. Porter was tall and thin, and his outfits were always very, very colorful and glistening. Since his band was called The Wagonmasters, most
of them had wagon wheel designs on them.

Although Dolly was one of several female singing partners Porter Wagoner had over the years, something was different with the two of them. They seemed like a perfect match. I could be wrong, but when I look at the many album covers Daddy did for them, it seemed like they didn't have to *act* as if they cared for each other. There was just something there, no acting required. This is just my observation.

For one of Dolly's album covers, Daddy had to photograph her husband. Carl Dean has done a great job of staying out of the limelight, and when I asked Daddy about him, he told me he was just a very private, quiet, nice guy.

A T.V. taping in Nashville in 1967. (l to r) Unidentified man, Marijohn Wilkins, Archie Campbell, Ed Bruce, Don Warden, Speck Rhodes, unidentified man, unidentified man, George Morgan, Dolly Parton, Porter Wagoner, unidentified man, George McCormick, Buck Trent, Ramona Jones, Grandpa Jones, and Frosty. PHOTOGRAPH BY LES LEVERETT.

Dolly and Porter performing on the set of *The Porter Wagoner Show* at the WSM studios in Nashville in 1968. PHOTOGRAPH BY LES LEVERETT.

Truly, the only stories I heard about Carl Dean, Dolly's husband, were about Daddy's work with him and a story about a trip to the grocery, which I heard only when I was an adult. The story had been floating around and retold by so many people by that time, I can only hope it wasn't real.

One night, Dolly and Carl ran out to the grocery together. Carl began looking at magazines. Dolly became impatient and told him that she would just go on and shop and meet him back at the magazine rack. She went about her business of finding everything on her grocery list and went back to meet up with Carl. There he stood, in the same spot as she had left him. She was overtaken by an urge to play a prank, so she slipped up behind him, put her hand between his legs, and "tweaked" his privates. It was then that she heard Carl laughing . . . from behind her. He had gone to look for her, so it was not Carl she had surprised. (I often wonder if that man now knows who grabbed him so inappropriately in the grocery store years ago.)

Daddy not only photographed shows, he also photographed many history-making recording sessions on Music Row. One of the most amazing things he ever saw in a recording session took place when Dolly Parton was in the studio. He was in the control booth with her and the engineers. They were doing a playback to fine-tune a song they had just cut. It was loud, very loud. Daddy says he looked over and there sat Dolly, writing another song. In that deafening, small room with the words of her last tune blaring through the speakers, she had the ability to totally block out everything around her and create.

Recording studios were always exciting to me. I knew very well not to utter a sound. Sometimes I sat in the smoky control booth as Daddy worked. Half-empty cups of thick, black coffee sat on every surface, and men with cigarettes and furrowed brows listened for things I could not even discern. Everything would be sounding just fine to me, and they would stop the musicians and start again. Over and over, to the point of tears, they would play the same song. They spoke to the musicians and the

(l to r) Chet Atkins, RCA producer Bob Ferguson, Shel Silverstein, Waylon Jennings, and Willie Nelson, in a recording studio before a Chet Atkins and Les Paul recording session in 1977. PHOTOGRAPH BY LES LEVERETT.

artist over a speaker and it sounded so odd. They would cut it on, talk to them, click it off, and sometimes say something derogatory. They would laugh where the people in the studio could see, but not hear. The same went on in the studio, where walls of wood and glass and tangles of wires and microphones took up the small space. It was all in good humor. The musicians always wore headphones, and I wondered if they were listening to the *Rolling Stones*, as my brothers did in their bedrooms. (I later learned they were not.)

Bob Ferguson was the producer of many of Dolly and Porter's recordings. He was not only a producer, but also a very prolific song-writer. He won the CMA song of the year in 1969 for "The Carroll County Accident" and also wrote the popular "Wings of a Dove." He also happened to be one of Daddy's dearest friends, and his children were some of my own favorite friends. Bob was part Native American and was married to a sweet Choctaw woman named Martha. She used to make native jewelry and dresses for my dolls.

Bob produced and did the makeup for the Porter Wagoner album, *Confessions of a Broken Man*, which won a Grammy award for Best Album Cover. Daddy says that they had a lot of fun shooting this cover, with Porter dressed in character as "Skid Row Joe." Later, Daddy did another cover for Porter with the same character for the album, *The Bottom of the Bottle*.

Through Bob, Daddy became a member of the Southeastern Indian Antiquities Survey (SIAS), a local branch of amateur archaeologists. I had always been fascinated with history and archaeology, so I went to many meetings with Daddy. Bob was always there, along with several

other music industry people. Every now and then, our friends, Tex Ritter and his son Tom, would sit with us as we listened to interesting lectures on topics such as the Woodland Indians.

When I was fifteen, I had the exciting adventure of actually working on a local dig, west of Nashville at Mound Bottom, a site that Vanderbilt University was excavating. SIAS members, including my daddy, my brothers, and I worked every Saturday of that summer, slowly uncovering prehistory. I was the only nonadult on the site.

As far as career goals, it was

A 1968 photograph of producer, Bob Ferguson, Porter Wagoner, and Les Leverett during a photograph session with Porter as his character, Skid row Joe. FROM THE COLLECTION OF LES LEVERETT.

a turning point for me. I had always known that I was meant for the creative arts, but archaeology was next on my list of interests. After many very hot, tiring days in the scorching sun and hours of never uncovering a major find, I knew that I should stick to "plan A." I decided to set my mind on recording current history for someone else to dig up in the future. Still, working at an actual site was a very educational experience and a wonderful time to share with my family and Bob Ferguson.

We shared many memorable occasions with Bob.

He once purchased an old log structure in Kentucky and asked Daddy to photograph it and help him number the logs and record numbers in preparation for moving the house. These two brave men set out, with Bob's two oldest children and me, on a cool autumn day to work on this

Porter Wagoner looking at himself in a bottle. This photo was made before computer magic during a photo session for the album cover, *Bottom of the Bottle* in 1968. PHOTOGRAPH BY LES LEVERETT.

The Mound Bottom archaeological dig west of Nashville in 1974. Bob Ferguson is in the foreground helping Libby dig her square. Libby's brother, John, is on the far left. PHOTOGRAPH BY LES LEVERETT.

project. While they were in the house, numbering logs, the three of us kids were running around, laughing, and yelling while romping in the autumn leaves. It must have been a major distraction for two men hopped up on coffee and trying to record numbers. Bob shouted out the window, "Hey, you kids calm down! You're acting like a bunch of wild Indians!" He had no sooner said it, than he realized that two-thirds of the kids he was fussing at were indeed Indians. He and Daddy looked at each other and cracked up laughing. Actually, I felt proud to be called a "wild Indian" because I thought his kids were cool. (I had always wanted my 1/32 of Indian blood to show more.)

Bob and Martha owned an old house on Linden Avenue in the Belmont area of Nashville. There was what seemed like hundreds of rooms in this huge house. They would entertain often, and many times my mom would go over to their house on the morning of those parties to help Martha and some of the other women get the house and the food ready. I recall maybe a dozen of us kids playing in that big house at one time. We would go from room to room and have the world's greatest games of hide-and-seek. Once, the ladies put us to work, cleaning up the yard and lawn furniture for an outside party. We ended up in a big water fight. In the hot sun that day, we were a rainbow of color, me the palest, the Ferguson kids with their lovely bronze skin, and a couple of our African American friends.

Bob and Martha Ferguson in front of their home in Nashville. PHOTOGRAPH BY LES LEVERETT.

(l to r) Dorothy Ritter, Dot Leverett, Rocky Top writer Boudleaux Bryant, and Choctaw Chief Phillip Martin at the Cheekwood Fine Arts Center in Nashville during a George Catlin exhibit and meeting of the SIAS in 1971. PHOTOGRAPH BY LES LEVERETT.

When the party began, people like Chet Atkins would be in the crowd, and we children would run between conversations to get to the food, then go sit on their grand staircase to eat while pretending to be at wedding parties or with royalty. What an unusual crowd, with music industry greats, professors from Vanderbilt University, and various members of the SIAS.

During my childhood summers, we would travel to Philadelphia, Mississippi, to attend the Choctaw Indian Fair. Through Bob Ferguson, Daddy was very involved in the culture at the Pearl River Reservation, and together they put out *The Chata Anumpa* newspaper on a regular basis. We would travel in a caravan from Nashville. Jerry Reed went down for entertainment, as did Connie Smith, Johnny Gimble, musicians Weldon Myrick, Pigg Robbins, and Bobby Dyson. I hung out with the Ferguson kids, and Weldon Myrick and Jerry Reed's daughters. After a long, hot day of viewing Choctaw crafts, sitting in the sun watching shows and stickball games, eating ethnic delights and riding rides, we would all meet up in the hotel pool for a swim.

One afternoon, we were invited to Martha's family reunion on the reservation. For the first hour, I thought that no one spoke English. I finally found out that we were the only white people ever invited to a Choctaw family reunion in Martha's childhood home. Her family was in shock, I guess. Bob told us that it was considered an honor. We had dishes with homemade hominy, fry bread, and chicken.

Bob's car broke down on one of these trips. The whole Ferguson family had to ride with us in our Pontiac all the way to Nashville. There were four adults and four children, one still nursing. The Ferguson's luggage traveled in the Myrick's station wagon as we caravanned home. It made for a very long, interesting, and unforgettable trip. We laughed a lot, yet I also had my first taste of discrimination on that journey. My family had introduced me to tolerance and ethnic diversity early in life, even though I didn't realize it.

I was only about ten at the time and had been around people from all backgrounds all my life. I never noticed differences . . . not even differences in attitudes toward nonwhite Americans. I never thought it odd that three white Leveretts were traveling with five Native Americans. But others along the way did. We stopped at more than a few restaurants before being served without glares and stares. Bob's daughter asked why everyone was staring and Weldon Myrick's wife, Kitty, replied, "They're looking at you because you are so beautiful." (Kitty was an angel.) If only it were that simple. Near the reservation, we had encountered restaurants where Native Americans would only be served through the drive-up windows. I didn't understand back then. Over thirty years later I still don't.

Mom had a secret going on with Bob's oldest son on the way back

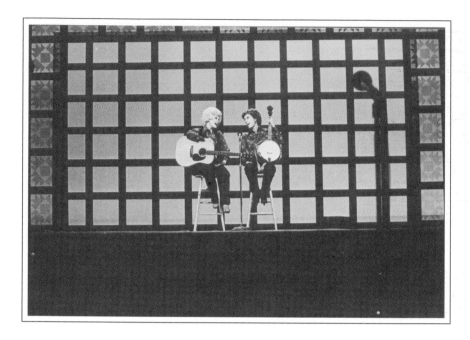

Dolly Parton and Carol Burnett at a taping at the Opry House in Nashville in 1978. PHOTOGRAPH BY LIBBY LEVERETT-CREW.

to Nashville. She told him that he could be the first to tell us when we were close to home by spotting the tall WSM radio tower. That tower made a very large statement on the outskirts of our city, and you could see it for miles. You could hear its signals even farther.

Back in Nashville, these tight circles of friends and acquaintances supported, inspired, and delighted me, and I have never been free of any of the lessons I have learned along the way, especially the most unexpected lessons.

When I grew up and began photographing jobs on my own, I had the pleasure of working with the same people that Daddy had worked with in his career. Since I had been around them all my life, I never felt like they were anything other than family, and my comfort level was the same.

Porter Wagoner called me and asked if I would photograph his performance at the Nashville Palace, a nightclub near the Opry House. I took the assignment and spent most of the night visiting with old family friends like Marty Stuart.

A funny thing happened when I delivered Porter's prints. He told me to just stick them in his mailbox at his home in Music Valley, and he would have my check in an envelope there waiting for me. I put the package in the box, and, unfortunately, the mail had already been delivered so I had to go through the mail to find my check. As I did so, I realized that the mail did not have Porter's name on it, but Mrs. Rudy, of Rudy's Farm Sausage fame. It was then that I noticed a lady, presumably, Mrs. Rudy, watching me from her window. I waved, took my package out of her mailbox, and went to the next, and correct, one. She watched me as I then, went through Porter's mail looking for my check and left the package. When I got home, I had to call Porter to tell him what had happened in case Mrs. Rudy wanted to know why I was digging in her mailbox. He laughed.

As an adult, I also worked with Dolly Parton at the CMA Awards show and once when she and Carol Burnett were filming a television show at the Opry House. She grabbed me, gave me a big hug, and said, "How in the world is Les? You tell him hello now, ya hear?" I felt seven years old again. Funny, I still feel that way a lot around the business, even with graying hair.

I keep expecting someone to pinch my cheek. I guess that's how it is with family.

A SMALL WORLD TOUR

There is something very nomadic about Bluegrass. It's not just the wandering, drifting genre of the music, but the lifestyle of its players and its followers. During my life in the music world, my extended family of friends and acquaintances seem to run in the same circles. No matter what style of music they are involved with, or what their association, we keep drifting into each other.

Roy Acuff with Sam Bush and Porter Wagoner at the Grand Masters Fiddling Contest at Opryland in Nashville in 1974. PHOTOGRAPH BY LES LEVERETT.

The Jones house during a picking and dance. Grandpa Jones is in the doorway. Pam Simmons is dancing, and Chet Atkins is watching from the right of the photo. PHOTOGRAPH BY LES LEVERETT.

One person introduces you to another and they in turn introduce you to someone else. People I knew through my nights with Daddy at the *Opry* when I was very young, reappear in my current life, in front of my own lens, or next to me at a party. The same people I saw at the *Opry*, I saw at the Ozark Folk Center in Mountain View, Arkansas, the Bluegrass Festival in Bean Blossom, Indiana, the Grand Masters Fiddling Contest in Nashville, at rock concerts, record label parties, and awards shows. I would see the same people at art show openings, ballets, recording sessions, symphony performances, baby showers, weddings, funerals, and in each other's homes.

When I was a teenager, one of my favorite places to be with friends was at Grandpa and Ramona Jones's home. The phones would start ringing up and down the line, and the next thing you knew, a pickin' had been planned at their house. These were festive occasions where everyone could just cut loose and have fun and socialize without microphones, television cameras, and crowds. When my daddy took photographs at these gatherings, he was not working.

John Hartford, Billy Ed Wheeler, Chet Atkins, Johnny Russell, Mac Wiseman, Eddie Stubbs, Oswald Kirby, Roy Acuff, Charlie Collins, Roland White, Charlie Cushman, Ruth McClain of the McClain Family, Marty Stuart, Buck, Sharon and Cheryl White, Joe and Rose Lee Maphis, Earl Scruggs, and Nat Winston would play in front of the fireplace. In front of them, someone would be calling a square dance. Another crowd of people were eating, drinking, and visiting in the kitchen. Sometimes, another group of musicians and singers would be playing another tune in the living room. It was a blend of folk, bluegrass, country, and love. The music brought us together on those cozy nights at the Joneses's, and somehow it gave us a bond thicker than blood.

There were friends there from *Hee Haw* as well as the *Grand Ole Opry*. The Joneses's had close ties with the Ozark Folk Center in Mountain View, Arkansas, and those players would make the long journey just for one of those impromptu gatherings.

Picking and dancing at the Joneses's. John Hartford and Ramona Jones play in the foreground Terry Smith is on upright bass, and Billy Smith is beyond Ramona. PHOTOGRAPH BY LES LEVERETT.

We went to Mountain View several times over the years. The Joneses eventually moved there for a while and would invite us out to see them. We traveled there, along with Merle Travis and The Whites, for their daughter's wedding. The music was different there. It was more mountain folk music. But I noticed the dance steps were the same and the people were some of the gentlest on earth. It is a lovely place.

I've been to some wonderful places because of my daddy's and my own work and the friendships we've made through it. What a wonderful thing, to record history, travel, and make lifetime friends at the same time.

Roy Acuff with Porter Wagoner presenting a thirteen-year-old Mark O'Connor an award for winning the Grand Masters Fiddling Contest in 1975. PHOTOGRAPH BY LES LEVERETT.

Being involved in recording history is a special honor. The first time Daddy photographed Mark O'Connor, he was thirteen and had just won the Grand Masters Fiddling Contest at Opryland. His mother found

Mark O'Connor playing in Roy Acuff's dressing room at the Opry House with Charlie Collins in 1983. PHOTOGRAPH BY LES LEVERETT.

Daddy's name on the back of the one print she had of him accepting his award, and she got in touch with him. They kept in contact for years as Mark's success grew.

My father had also watched Marty Stuart grow up in the music business. Marty Stuart, his sister Jennifer, and his parents became friends of ours through the Joneses, although Daddy had photographed him from the time he first came to town to play with Lester Flatt. When I was older and took a course in studio photography, Marty went to class with me as my model. Ever so witty, my daddy and I have some great images of him that we joke about saving for bribes.

Marty and I always have this little comedic conversation when we see each other. One of us says, "Not a dern thing and he doesn't start that 'til a noon." We are quoting our beloved Grandpa Jones's onetime reply when asked how his son, Mark, was doing. We laugh and laugh and then try to come up with other Grandpa quotes and funny memories of times together.

Grandpa Jones, Joe and Rose Lee Maphis, and Ramona Jones backstage at the Ryman in 1972. PHOTOGRAPH BY LES LEVERETT.

Mark Jones and Dale Maphis (the son of Joe and Rose Lee Maphis) also grew up in the backstage areas of the entertainment world. It's said that when Dale and Mark were infants and the Joneses and Maphises were doing a show together, they used their empty guitar cases on the side of the stage as baby cribs.

I never slept in a guitar case, but at many shows, I did my fair share of time backstage sleeping up against Daddy's camera bag.

When I was still in high school, I shot my first professional photographic job. It was for George Hamilton IV and consisted of capturing on film a sign with his name in lights. It wasn't much in the creative department, but nonetheless, my first job. My next job quickly followed and was a little more interesting. Mark and Dale made an album with second-generation musicians and me, the second-generation photographer, taking the cover shot. They picked me up after school, and my mother saw me go off in a van full of crazy boys. She laughed, but I don't think she would have if she hadn't known them.

Years before the photo shoot with those wild boys, Oscar Sullivan of Lonzo and Oscar, and his wife, Geneva, had a wonderful hayride at their home in the country. Alisa Jones and I hung out together all evening in our cool tie-dyed, elephant-leg pants with matching vests. We rode out to a spot in the woods where a huge kettle of stew hung over a big fire. Tables were stacked high with other food and drinks. While the adults visited, the teenagers and kids took turns swinging on an old grapevine. Alisa and I really had our eye on Dale that night. Back then to us, he was cute beyond words. He went way out on that vine, swung back right into the tree, and went splash in the mud. So much for making the girls swoon. That night, on the hayride back to our cars, Merle Travis, Grandpa, and Joe Maphis were sitting behind us kids singing loudly and laughing. I had no idea I was near such treasures.

So many from that generation of entertainers are now gone. I didn't know that some of the younger ones would leave so soon, too. Dale Maphis died in a car accident in 1989. Roy Husky Jr. also died young. He had always been around the *Opry*, another member of the unofficial second-generation bunch of music kids. His instrument of choice was the upright bass. I always got tickled when I heard that instrument referred to as a "dog house" bass, although it sure fit. I think a dog could have a litter in one and still have room to turn around. Sometimes Roy would catch a ride with Del Wood over to work at the Ryman. She drove a big, long station wagon. Del was a full-figured woman, and he was a toothpick of a guy, young enough to be her son. They were quite the sight coming in the backstage door together with that big old bass and her bag of makeup. Roy was quiet, but he always smiled, spoke, and loved good humor.

Marty Stuart once filmed a music video, on which I was hired as the still photographer. Roy Husky Jr. was playing upright bass on the set, and he was holding a cigar in his mouth as he played. As they shot and reshot the scene, the cigar had to be replaced with one of the same length to keep consistency in the film. It became comical after a while. At one point, they kept rolling film and his cigar burned down to his lips. The

(l to r), Camera crew, Marty, W. S. Holland, and Roy Husky Jr. on the set of a video shoot for a Marty Stuart song. PHOTOGRAPH BY LIBBY LEVERETT-CREW.

closer it got to his mouth, the wider his smile got until he could no longer hold it in his teeth. Marty doesn't just chuckle when he laughs. He has a full body laugh, and once he got started, the whole film crew cracked up.

Through Marty, I met Manuel. He is connected to the music business literally by a thread. Manuel is a clothier who has kept the rhinestones shining in Nashville for years. His rhinestone and sequined Western-type outfits are each handmade and a work of art. He has designed clothes for everyone from Johnny Cash to Riders in the Sky to Elvis. He started out working at Nudie's Rodeo Tailor in Hollywood, California. When he first opened his shop in Nashville, he asked me to photograph the grand opening. And it *was* grand. Porter Wagoner, Emmylou Harris, Sylvester Stallone's mother, and Marty and his sister, Jennifer Stuart, were some of Manuel's customers and supporters who showed up for his opening.

I went to Manuel's home, south of Nashville, to photograph parties, and even a family wedding. He has a lovely log home, high up on a hill

Emmylou Harris, Manuel, and Porter Wagoner at Manuel's in Nashville in 1989.
PHOTOGRAPH BY LIBBY LEVERETT-CREW.

with a magnificent view and trees all around. The first time I went to
his home, he and Jennifer Stuart were sitting in a swing out under a
huge oak tree. They were laughing because they had been watching me,
down below, making wrong turns on the small country roads, and going
back and forth before I found the right drive. Being the charming gentleman that he is, he offered me his spot and stood visiting with us as I
loaded my cameras. He never treated me as if I were a worker. He
treated everyone from the caterer, to the waiters, to the valet parking
attendants, to the guest of honor the very same way. Drinks, food, and
good conversation were plentiful, and with his generosity and polite
manner, you left Manuel's parties with a warm feeling. It was akin to a
family reunion.

Marty Stuart and Manuel at a post-CMA Awards Show party in Nashville.
PHOTOGRAPH BY LIBBY LEVERETT-CREW.

Every Bluegrass event is like a family reunion. When the International Bluegrass Music Museum opened in Owensboro, Kentucky, they asked my father to prepare an exhibit of his favorite Bluegrass images. He didn't know where to start. They were all his favorites.

142

Les Leverett giving a talk during a seminar at the International Bluegrass Music Museum in Owensboro, Kentucky, in 1994. PHOTOGRAPH BY LIBBY LEVERETT-CREW.

Completed, it was a lovely show and they even invited him to participate in a seminar at the opening. Dr. Tom Adler, director of the museum, told him he had to talk for forty-five minutes. He said he couldn't do it.

I went up for the festivities and to hear Daddy's speech. At the end of forty-five minutes, Daddy looked to the back at the room and there stood Dr. Adler waving his arms and pointing at his watch. Daddy ended it soon, before he was through. Back at the hotel, Alison Krauss, and other Bluegrass greats were playing in the lobby, on the stairs, in the corners and even on the elevator at the hotel. While there, I realized that Bluegrass artists just couldn't help themselves. They get a song in their head and they have to play it, no matter where they are. Someone else joins in and the next thing you know, there's a crowd and it's four hours later.

Bean Blossom in 1970. PHOTOGRAPH BY LES LEVERETT.

(l to r) Dot Leverett, Libby Leverett, Norman Blake, unidentified musician, Tut Taylor, and Pete Sayers of England at Bean Blossom. PHOTOGRAPH BY LES LEVERETT.

Years after that opening, Daddy was surprised, in 2001, when the International Bluegrass Music Association awarded him their Distinguished Achievement Award for his promotion of Bluegrass through his photography. It was a very big honor and very well deserved since he had been photographing and following Bluegrass for so many years.

When I was about ten, I went along with my parents to Bean Blossom, Indiana, to the Bean Blossom Bluegrass Festival. It was beyond warm that summer week. It was hot. Not just the weather, but the music, too. Daddy had to photograph the event, so Mom and I would stretch out on a blanket under a shade tree, fan ourselves with folded programs, drink cold drinks, and just observe. It was so dry, there was an orange dust all around.

It stuck to our sweaty bodies, and when I got in the tub that night the water turned to mud.

I had never been to a music festival before. It's said my brother's friends had snuck off to Woodstock and another rock festival in Atlanta. I heard some tales about those festivals, but this was a first for me. Funny, but I think the crowds were similar in many ways. I had never seen so many people and instruments and little groups of musicians interspersed throughout the fields of cars and tents and campers. The main event seemed secondary to what was going on around us. People were there from all over the world. Although I was used to seeing many of these people back home in Nashville, they looked different in this setting. I remember Norman Blake with sweat dripping from his hair. He looked like he had just stepped out of a shower where he had worn all his clothes. Bill Monroe, "The Father of Bluegrass," was there watching over his children.

Bill Monroe onstage at Bean Blossom in 1970. PHOTOGRAPH BY LES LEVERETT.

Bill Monroe performing on the *Opry* in 1987. PHOTOGRAPH BY LIBBY LEVERETT-CREW.

There were some people from my childhood I never knew how to "read," so I treaded lightly around them. Bill Monroe was one of those people. He was tall and mysterious. I'd see him smile sweetly, and then he'd stare at me harshly. I later learned that he was not judging me, nor was he turning me away, he was just off in another place, not even thinking of what he was saying or doing, undoubtedly with a fiddle tune bouncing around in his head.

He looked tidy in his gray suit and tie and his cowboy hat. The hat was white, so I presumed he was a good guy. Wherever he was, there was a group always around him, carrying instruments and usually playing. Bluegrass lovers were in awe of the man. Bluegrass musicians held him right up there, one notch down from God himself. Some of them hauled hay on his farm for little or nothing, just to be in his presence.

During my childhood, Bill Monroe was one of those people who was just always there. Daddy used to go out to his farm to photograph and sometimes just to visit. Dr. Adler had asked Bill to come up to the

Bill Monroe and Emmylou Harris performing on the *Opry* the night of Bill's fiftieth *Opry* anniversary in 1989. PHOTOGRAPH BY LES LEVERETT.

Les and Bill Monroe backstage at the Opry House in 1989. FROM THE COLLECTION OF LES LEVERETT.

Bluegrass Museum, and Bill told him he would not come unless Les Leverett would go with him. Daddy says that he doesn't know if he wanted him to go with him because he wanted him to take photographs or if he just wanted the company. Daddy ended up going up with him, a couple of other friends, and my mom. Andy Owens, who was also a Bluegrass musician, flew in from Dallas to drive them up in Bill's limousine. It was an eventful day, with that limousine overheating along the way and Bill handing out quarters to children at a restaurant where they had lunch.

The last time I saw Bill Monroe was at a record label party. I was photographing the event for the label, and that evening Al Gore was in

George Strait and Bill Monroe at a post-CMA Awards Show party in Nashville in 1987. PHOTOGRAPH BY LIBBY LEVERETT-CREW.

town making the rounds. He showed up at the party, and Bill watched but never asked me to take a photo of them together. Everyone else did though. Bill looked lonely that night. He didn't have his usual following of people.

Feeling sorry for him, I chatted for a while. There was this running joke that our families were related. He sang a song about his Uncle Pen Vandiver. Supposedly, this was the same Pen Vandiver who was a very distant relative of my mother's family. Dad would joke with Mom that she and Bill were cousins. It worried me that he looked so lonely that night, until I realized what was missing . . . his mandolin. He just looked completely lost and alone without it. It was attached to his very soul, and without it, he was not complete.

For many years, two youngsters you would find not far from Bill's shadow were Billy and Terry Smith. They had moved to Nashville with their songwriting mother, Hazel, in 1969 and were eager to play and learn. They quickly became a part of our circle of friends in the music

Terry, Hazel, and Billy Smith in 1974. PHOTOGRAPH BY LES LEVERETT.

industry. The Smiths only lived about a mile away, so Hazel would drop in every so often with the boys. They were close to my age. Although I was going through a rock 'n' roll stage, I was fascinated with Billy and Terry and their love of and dedication to Bluegrass music. Hazel Smith was dedicated to and would do anything to help her children, and anyone else for that matter. She has had her share of hard knocks in the music business and never forgets a kindness. Her walls are lined with gold albums, trophies for songs she has written that have sold millions for Dr. Hook and Tammy Wynette among others. She has run Ricky Skaggs's office, managed her sons' careers as the Smith Brothers, and has worked with Tompall Glaser. She wrote for *Country Music Magazine* and is a radio correspondent. In 1999, she won the CMA's Media Achievement Award for her contribution to the promotion, and I shall add, the love, of country music.

Hazel is one of the best journalists. She always knows what's going on in the "business" in Nashville. I always joke that I cannot do a thing in Nashville without her knowing about it. It seems like every job I shoot in the music business, I run into Hazel. It's not a bad thing, but it is truly amazing, her ability to seem like she's in about ten places at one time. No wonder she's so good at what she does. Not only a big supporter of music, she supports her friends. When there's a death or serious illness, she is there. When there's cause for celebration, she is there.

Wherever Hazel is, she is the life of the party with humor rolling off her tongue like poetry. My friends gave me a lingerie shower when I married. I received an innocently lovely gown from John and Marie Hartford and a very tomboyish sleep shirt from someone else. Then I opened Hazel's gift. It was a very, very tiny and sexy, hot pink negligee with matching tiny panties. I blushed. She then announced to the whole giggling pack of women that she had taken her son, Billy, shopping with her because she needed to know what turned a man on in that department.

The Whites and Jerry Douglas backstage at Fan Fair in 1982. PHOTOGRAPH BY LES LEVERETT.

Ricky Skaggs, Sharon White, and Cheryl White performing on the *Opry* in 1980.
PHOTOGRAPH BY LES LEVERETT.

No one appreciated Hazel's humor as much as the Whites. Hazel had taken them all under her wing and cared for them like a sweet old great aunt. Buck and Pat moved to Nashville from Texas and gave the world four wonderful girls, all of them talented and as sweet as sugar. The Whites performed on the *Opry* and eventually moved on to more fame in the Coen brothers' feature film *O, Brother, Where Art Thou?* I hesitate to use the word *fame*, simply because I know they don't like that. The Whites are as down-home and humble as you can get. When Sharon was asked what she said to George Clooney when she met him on the movie set, she reminded us that she was dressed up as her character, an older singer in the thirties. She said to him, "I usually look better than this." That's why I have always loved the Whites. They are the real deal. What you see is what you get, and that family is wonderfully real. Sharon and Cheryl, along with their father, have been the backbone of the Whites, with Rosie and sometimes Melissa's help. They are some of my favorite people in the world. When Pat died, instead of a sad ceremony, the girls, Buck and Ricky Skaggs, Sharon's husband, gave her a musical send-off. Vince Gill, Marty Stuart, and Connie Smith sang. The girls talked. Other loved ones talked. Buck clogged. What else could they do? Everyone there was very sad, yet touched by Pat and her wonderful family.

Ricky Skaggs and Sharon White Skaggs in their dressing room backstage at the Opry House in 1982. PHOTOGRAPH BY LES LEVERETT.

The small world of the music industry, which sometimes could seem large and impersonal, was anything but. We were brought together in times of death and in times of joy. We were brought together over and over for reasons and in situations that none of us could explain.

Melissa White worked at a gym where I used to work out. Her husband is the son of *Opry* band member, Spider Wilson. At the same gym, I often saw and visited with Bob Boatman who was a good friend and the director of *Hee Haw*. I took dance lessons with Ernest Tubb's granddaughters. I was in school with Webb Pierce's son and Anita Carter's daughter. My playmate Sally Smathers now works for Dolly Parton. The school safety patrolwoman in a suburb I once drove through regularly was Roy Acuff's significant other. My first-grade boyfriend, Gordon Kennedy, the son of guitarist Jerry, won a Grammy for a song he co-wrote that Eric Clapton recorded. Ricky Skaggs recorded one of Carl Butler's songs. The circle just keeps on going, spiraling, and coming back on itself just like a bluegrass fiddle melody.

I was weaving in and out of a very colorful tapestry. Some areas looked very different from others. There were contrasts, yet everything was connected together by the fundamental love of music, people, and life in general. The threads that bind cross over each other, touching, yet moving away, only to come back and touch again.

And the first stitch was sewn at the *Opry*, many years ago.

THE STORM AT
HURRICANE MILLS

Born into the dark, coal-mining world of hard work and low wages, Loretta Webb Lynn had come out of the hills of Kentucky like the first flower of spring. With a strong twang and good lungs, stardom took hold, and before she knew it her name was a household word. Loretta Lynn became synonymous with country music.

Loretta Lynn performing on the *Opry* at the Ryman with Ernest Tubb in 1969.
PHOTOGRAPH BY LES LEVERETT.

Loretta Lynn being named a member of the *Grand Ole Opry* by *Opry* manager, Ott Devine in 1962. PHOTOGRAPH BY LES LEVERETT.

As a child I was thrilled to have company of any kind. There was just something about having a new adventure. I was so used to having interesting people around that if things got quiet around the house I asked my parents, almost begged them, to have company. I liked to listen to the conversations, songs, and laughter and thrived on the warm sensations of coffee brewing and everyone greeting with hugs and kisses. I would watch Mom get out the snack food and dishes. Everybody sat around the kitchen table to visit. They would talk and tell jokes and eventually someone would get out a guitar and sing. Sometimes they would play cards. I have no doubt that the neighbors could hear the uproarious laughter carrying through the screen door and open windows in the summer. In the winter, it just seemed to make the whole house bulge.

One Saturday, when the roads were covered in snow and ice, there was a knock on the door. Momma and Daddy just figured it was a neighbor, since no one in their right mind would be out driving on those dangerous streets. Daddy opened the door and there stood Doolittle Lynn, Loretta Lynn's husband. Daddy said, "Doo! What are you doing out on a day like this?" Doo replied, "Just seeing if I could drive." Daddy told him he looked and smelled like he was "set for forty below" and asked him to come in for a cup of coffee.

Mom had just taken an apricot nectar cake from the oven and asked if he would like a piece. He told her that he had never cared for cake, but thanks anyway. After sitting there visiting with Momma and Daddy for quite some time, and smelling that sweet cake, he finally gave in and decided to try a piece. The man who did not like cake ended up eating half of it. Maybe it helped sober him up. Daddy sent him on his way when he felt like Doo was okay to drive.

Soon after, the phone rang. It was Loretta. She wanted to know what kind of cake Mom had made that Doo was raving about. Mom told her all about it, and Loretta wanted the recipe. Mom said she'd mail it to her. She told her not to, that she would just come by for it one day soon when the roads cleared. Well, she showed up the next day to get the recipe and visited for a good while. After she left, my parents noticed she had left her purse and the recipe. They called to let her know, and she told them to just keep it and she would come by for it in a few days. So, Loretta left her purse just like that, for a few days.

Loretta was so trusting, so very country, and never acted like anyone but herself. I had no idea that people paid money to go hear her sing. To me, she was no different from the dry cleaning man who used to come by once a week. He didn't sing, but I just didn't think about it. I did notice that I didn't see him on Saturday nights at the *Opry,* but I did see Loretta and her good friend Patsy Cline.

I was only three years old when Patsy stopped showing up at the *Opry.* It was years before I learned that she had died in a plane crash. I

Loretta in her home with the twins, Peggy and Patsy, in 1965. Les also photographed the portrait on the wall behind her. PHOTOGRAPH BY LES LEVERETT.

(l to r) Jack Lynn (Loretta's son) Loretta, Teddy Wilburn, Jean Shepard, and Doyle Wilburn at the Loretta Lynn Rodeo in 1965. PHOTOGRAPH BY LES LEVERETT.

sensed sadness around the house and at the Ryman during that time, but I really didn't know why or what was going on. I guess I was being protected from the awful event.

Loretta and Doo lived near us on a big farm when they first moved to Nashville. In the middle of their living room was a huge tree that went from floor to ceiling. I guess it was cedar. It had all these little sawed-off branches on it and that was where everyone hung their hats and coats.

They also had an arena where they broke wild horses. Eventually, it became the Loretta Lynn Longhorn Rodeo. I have faint memories of going there to watch the "cowboys" and the horses. I liked to see the horses. I loved horses, but the bulls and the clowns frightened me. I remember Loretta being there, like everyone else . . . no airs, no large ego, just Loretta. She usually performed at her rodeo, and the fact that she was there brought in a large audience. Eventually, they sold their rodeo to Bruce Lehrke, and it became The Longhorn Championship Rodeo.

We used to go to Bruce's ranch to a big chuck wagon meal the week before the rodeo every year. There, we'd get to try new and exotic foods like buffalo stew. Entertainment was usually someone like Riders in the Sky. It was wonderful, but nothing like being at Loretta's.

One night, after the rodeo at Loretta's, one of the Wilburn Brothers introduced her to a gentleman from Vanderbilt University. After he left, she learned the man was a professor of English. Loretta shouted, "Good God a' mighty, why didn't you tell me and I'd a used one of them there ten-dollar words on 'em!" She was so funny.

Before they sold the rodeo, Loretta had told my mom about a turkey farm that was near their place. For some reason, Mom thought it would be good for me to go with her to choose our Thanksgiving dinner one year. I was excited to go see any kind of animal. I just loved critters and I thought I was going to get to pet them and run with them. I didn't know that turkeys were so mean. I had no idea that the turkey we were choosing was not for a pet, but was meant for the oven. I endured watching a lady ring the turkey's neck, gut it, pluck the feathers, and package that baby up for us to put in our car to bring home to cook. I had never been so distressed. Every time we went out to the Lynn's after that, I feared that we were going to stop by that nasty turkey farm.

Not long after Patsy Cline's death and the sale of the rodeo, Loretta and Doo bought a huge estate southwest of town at Hurricane Mills and that's what they called their new place—Hurricane Mills. It always seemed to be under construction and repair, but it was grand. A southern plantation home, it had tall ceilings, wonderful staircases, and big rooms. And, of course, no southern plantation would be complete without long, wide wrap-around porches.

Loretta and Doo had several kids, but I always hung out with the twins, Patsy and Peggy. They were younger than I was, but they were the ringleaders when it came to mischief. Things that I knew were wrong and inappropriate became okay when I was with them. We ran wild around Hurricane Mills. I had never had so much unattended freedom in my life. It always felt great until Doo got a hold of us.

Daddy had to photograph Loretta for an album cover. Mom and I went with him, together with Doyle Wilburn and his daughter. When we arrived, Doo just left what he was doing, which was caulking windows. What a big mistake. There, on the upstairs porch was a caulking gun with a full container of caulk attached. By the time he remembered what he was doing when we arrived, the twins and I had "caulked" all the windows, the doorframes, the railings, each other, and anything else we could find. We had written our names in caulk on the windowpanes. We had even located another container of caulking and figured out how to remove the old one and attach the new one. We were right proud of ourselves.

Doo, Peggy, Patsy, and Loretta at Hurricane Mills in 1969. PHOTOGRAPH BY LES LEVERETT.

Loretta Lynn at her Hurricane Mills home in 1969. PHOTOGRAPH BY LES LEVERETT.

I had never seen an adult so mad in my life. Doo's face turned red and he spoke pretty loud, using words I had never heard before, as he fussed at us. He aimed his anger more at the twins I guess, since I was company. He made us clean up the mess, which made a larger one. My greatest fear was of how disappointed my parents were going to be when he went back downstairs to let them know what I had done.

When we went downstairs, a little while later, I sat down with my tail tucked, expecting my parents to be angry and Doo's face to still be red. Instead, he winked at me. His girls had gone on as if it were nothing. I realized that he had not uttered a word about what had happened. I went from fearing Doo to really respecting him in a different way, although from that point on I kept my distance.

Banished from the house, we would run all over Hurricane Mills through fields of weeds and grain. They had chickens and roosters, and I loved to hang on the fence and just watch them pecking around in the dust. The twins would tell me stories about how chickens ate ticks and we

Loretta inside the Hurricane Mills home in 1969. That's Libby in the background outside.
PHOTOGRAPH BY LES LEVERETT.

Loretta in her kitchen at Hurricane Mills in 1969. PHOTOGRAPH BY LES LEVERETT.

ate chickens, so we must eat ticks too. Between the turkey farm and the tick story, I became a vegetarian for about a week after that.

I once watched Loretta pull her older daughter's hair back into a ponytail and brush it out in a loving manner. For some reason that memory stays with me. It was so real, so very normal, and maternal. All the other girls in the room were around her, watching, and everyone was talking at the same time. We were up in one of the large rooms in that big house. The older kids had told me there was a secret passage leading through a closet door to the downstairs, and I didn't know if they were joking with me. I kept looking to Loretta for verification. She would just glance over and smile, going along with whatever the kids were talking about.

That must have been easy for her. She grew up helping with so many "youngins" as she called them, that maternal love came easy. She felt normal around crowds, kids, and household chores.

My best recollections of Loretta at Hurricane Mills were of her in the kitchen visiting with my mom and getting ready for the photo shoot. It was to be taken there, in her kitchen. There was something very child-like about her, her southern drawl was one of the best, and I loved to hear her talk. She had on jeans with a bandana on her hair, looking every bit the part of a country girl.

Then I'd see her at the *Opry*. She was no different from the Loretta in the kitchen at Hurricane Mills; she'd just be dressed up. When Loretta Lynn showed up at the Ryman to perform on the *Grand Ole Opry*, she put on no airs. Sure, she dressed up in her nice stage dresses and high heels, but she was still down to earth. Her long black hair was teased up

Loretta doing dishes at Hurricane Mills in 1969. PHOTOGRAPH BY LES LEVERETT.

Loretta and Doolittle Lynn at Patsy Cline's home in 1965. PHOTOGRAPH BY LES LEVERETT.

on top of her head and lay loosely down her back and around the front of her neck, and she wore makeup for the stage. But when Loretta opened her mouth to speak, she was just that same old Loretta.

All of the female singers at the Ryman had to dress and put on their makeup in the ladies' room right beyond the backstage door. There were only a few stalls, and there were always bags of undergarments, shoes, and boxes sitting around on the floor, and clothes draped over the stall doors. Loretta or Wilma Lee Cooper or Kitty Wells, putting on their makeup, usually took up both sinks and mirrors. Mom had trained me to not get in the way when I went to the restroom at the Ryman. Little girls love dress-up though, and I loved looking at all the pretty dresses hanging over the doors.

Libby Leverett holding Del Wood's dog as she plays her piano in her home in Nashville. PHOTOGRAPH BY LES LEVERETT.

I remember watching Del Wood put on her lipstick. She played the piano, and her hit was, "Down Yonder." When she played, her hands bounced all over the keys, and she made it look so easy. She would turn her head and smile at her audience, never missing a note.

We went to Del's house in East Nashville a lot in my childhood. She had a son close to my age. When the two of us were old enough to work a summer job, we worked across from each other at the Opryland theme park. The Woods always had little dogs, and I loved to play with them on their stairwell. Del could not stay away from her piano. I remember her playing every time we went to visit, and I remember her popcorn. I am a popcorn junkie, so that memory always stands out in my mind. She actually popped it with peanuts. It was wonderfully delicious, but when we tried it at home, it never worked right. I suppose she was magical not only with the piano, but also with her popcorn.

Del made me want to keep up with my piano lessons. Then again, I wanted to take photographs like Daddy. I wanted to do art like my mom. I wanted to study archaeology. I wanted to act. I wanted to dance. There was just so much to do in this life!

When I was a young adult, I decided that I would just try my hand at acting. My first job was as an extra in a film with Jerry Reed. I spent a whole day in the blazing sun only to walk across the sidewalk in front of the camera with a dozen other people. That was it. No lines, nothing. To top things off, that scene was cut from the movie.

My second, and last, role came soon after when I was cast with about a hundred other people as an extra in *Coalminer's Daughter*, the film about Loretta Lynn's life. Sissy Spacek played Loretta, and Tommy Lee Jones played the part of Doo. In one scene, I was next to Tommy Lee Jones. I watched him going over his lines and pacing nervously before the film rolled. He spoke to me and I wondered who in the heck he was. (Who would've known?) Again, most of my scenes were cut. I took it as an omen that I was never meant for acting.

Loretta Lynn and actress Sissy Spacek backstage at the Opry in 1979. Sissy played the role of Loretta in *Coalminer's Daughter*. PHOTOGRAPH BY LES LEVERETT.

It's funny how a lot of people only know Loretta Lynn's story through the movie. They picture her looking like Sissy Spacek and Doo looking like Tommy Lee Jones.

Although Loretta was used to the stage and to working with crowds, she was so naïve that she did things that would be very embarrassing to most people, but she was so naïve that she didn't know she should be embarrassed. One night at the *Opry*, she noticed that the Japanese ambassador and some of his Japanese friends whom she had met back-stage were sitting on the front row during her set. After her song, she decided to introduce them to the audience, (which went out over the airwaves to millions of households). She said something to the effect

Loretta Lynn and actress Sissy Spacek backstage at the Opry House with *Grand Ole Opry* member Skeeter Davis in 1979. PHOTOGRAPH BY LES LEVERETT.

Loretta being interviewed by Cousin Ray of WPWC Radio in 1982. She is pointing at and speaking to Les. PHOTOGRAPH BY LES LEVERETT.

that the Japanese ambassador was in the audience and that they were the ones who "bummed" Pearl Harbor. As Daddy says, she's not Emily Post. She is simply Loretta. What you see is what you get.

I photographed Loretta a few times in my own career. I don't think she ever remembered my first name, but she knew I was Les Leverett's daughter and would always ask about him and Mom.

Many times, Daddy would be out front photographing her on the *Opry* stage and she would yell "Les!" in between verses, even on the live TV segment. In her childlike ways, she never thought before she said anything. I guess that's why we love her.

TAPS ON THE PLYWOOD, BOATS ON THE RIVER

It must have been fate that got me out of the house to go to John Hartford's one cold, December night. I had been away, living in Colorado trying to find myself and had come home without me. I hadn't given up the search, but I was back where I had started, among all the music people of my life.

Although I totally lacked musical talent, it seemed that music followed me wherever I went. On my first great adventure away from the security of my home in Nashville, I was still in the middle of it.

In my early twenties, I applied for a job in Colorado at the YMCA of the Rockies in Estes Park, about seventy miles northwest of Denver, and about fifty miles south of Cheyenne, Wyoming. It was not an easy job to come by, and I was very privileged to have been accepted there for two seasons. The Y was in a picturesque location, nestled in the heart of the Rocky Mountains, bordering on the Rocky Mountain National Park. The air was crisp, cool, and clean and the mountains showed a different face every day. I cleaned toilets for the honor of getting to hike and live in those mountains.

When I prepared to leave Nashville, I went backstage at the Opry House one last time. At that point, I hoped that I would find myself and stay in the mountains. I really didn't know if I was coming back. So I had to say goodbye to my old stomping grounds and the people who had shared them with me. That night on the *Opry*, the Vic Willis Trio dedicated and sang *Colorado* to me. I cried like a baby. My heart was pulling me away to explore other places, yet my heart was also right

Libby with the Vic Willis Trio on the *Opry* stage in 1981. PHOTOGRAPH BY LES LEVERETT.

Libby with Bashful Brother Oswald dancing on the *Opry* stage in 1965. PHOTOGRAPH BY LES LEVERETT.

there, with all of those people I had known all my life. No one made it easy on me.

One of Roy's Acuff's band members, "Bashful Brother Oswald" couldn't stop hugging me. He had seen me grow up backstage and couldn't believe I was ready to go off on my own. Os wore overalls, a floppy hat, and big clown shoes. When I was a little girl at the Ryman, he would come over to the side of the stage where I would sometimes

Libby with Oswald and Roy Acuff in their dressing room backstage at the Opry House in 1981. PHOTOGRAPH BY LES LEVERETT.

stand while Daddy was working, and he would scoop me up into his arms and dance me out onto the stage under the bright spotlights. I always wondered why someone who could dance on a stage with really big shoes would be called "bashful." Over the years, when I was indeed feeling bashful myself, I would see him spot me and I would sink into the background and out of his reach. This became our little game. Some nights I would give in and take the glory of the stage, but mostly, I chose to sit out, especially when I was a teenager.

Everyone used to congregate in Roy's dressing room backstage, across from the green room. He left the door open most of the time, and there was always a crowd in there. Minnie would be in there telling jokes. Roy's entire band was there and if a big name dropped by, the visitor would be there, too. It was like a hospitality stop. The walls of Roy's dressing room were lined with photographs of many people he had met in his career and the people he was around all the time. My daddy had taken most of them. There was one of him and Daddy together and even one of Roy and me together on his wall.

Many times when someone was in concert at the Opry House, they would use his dressing room. In later years, I had an assignment to photograph Blues guitarist, Stevie Ray Vaughn. The photo session took place in Roy's dressing room. It felt so odd that night to be in that dressing room without Roy there . . . especially with a Blues artist.

My brother Gary is a stagehand and worked at the Opry House. Years later, when Roy had been gone for a long time, my brother was snowed in while working a show. He slept that night in Roy's dressing room. I knew that he felt warm and safe surrounded by the many memories and the spirits in that once noisy room.

I was with Roy in his dressing room on my last night at the *Opry* before flying out to Colorado. He was sad that I was going and told me

Actors Joseph Campanello and Jack Albertson, Roy Acuff, Libby, and Vanessa Redgrave, unidentified woman, and Jerry Strobel, house manager of the *Opry*, in Roy's dressing room at the Opry in 1981. PHOTOGRAPH BY LES LEVERETT.

John Hartford performing on the *Opry* in 1978. PHOTOGRAPH BY LES LEVERETT.

I better come back. He reminded me not to meet any old boys who would take me away from the *Opry*. That night, actors Vanessa Redgrave and Jack Albertson were in town and hanging around with Roy. Vanessa got wind of our conversation and after introductions and photos, she pulled me over to the side. She told me that she had enjoyed watching me with my daddy and that she had also followed her father's example and was very close to him. She reminded me of the riches around me. I listened, but I already knew what she meant.

Once I got to Colorado, I was so busy with my new friends and exploring every mountain trail possible that my old life seemed very far away. It was not. In reality, it was close by.

I took my friends backstage to a Charlie Daniels concert in Cheyenne, Wyoming, guests of some musician friends back home. I took them backstage to a John Hartford concert at Chautauqua near Boulder, Colorado. We went to shows at Red Rocks, outside Denver. But one concert stands out, and not really the concert but a conversation while I was there.

I got a phone call at the Y one day from John Hartford's wife, Marie. She had heard from Mom that I was in Colorado and wanted me to know that John was going to be on the road and performing nearby at Red Rocks. They would love for me to come out and see the show and would arrange backstage passes for four.

Road trip! My friends were elated to have another backstage experience, and I was delighted to see some familiar faces from home. We piled into my best friend Alice's tiny, bright yellow Honda and zoomed off on the winding roads to Red Rocks. Things I had grown used to, such as backstage passes and backstage doors and feeling a part of the energy of a show, were very exciting to my friends. It was fun to share in their excitement. We had raided the kitchen at our camp before setting off and stuffed ourselves with fresh radishes and party mix. It was a deadly combination and we still laugh about our unladylike belches that evening.

Our passes were waiting at the door, and we roamed around backstage. We finally found John behind the set. John had always been a mysterious person. He was a very deep thinker, and when you spoke with him, you got the feeling that he wasn't really listening because his mind was racing trying to capture all the lyrics and tunes in his head. He was never very talkative with me, but this night was different. I don't know if it was because he was away from familiar turf or because it was just a mood he was in or if he had realized I was now an adult and he could talk more freely, but he really opened up to me that night. My friends had found a place on the side of the stage to watch the opening acts, and I remained with John.

Other times when we talked, John was shuffling his feet or playing with his bow. This night, he was standing still. His fiddle and bow tucked safely in its case, his arms folded over his chest. The plywood that he danced on as he played was already on the stage. He asked how my summer was going and how it was to be away from home. I shared with him how intense everything was, from the experience of being in the mountains to the way my new friendships were forming. We talked about relationships and heartbreaks. He reminded me that was what made the right one sweet. I told him about all the neat things I had seen hiking in the Rockies. We talked about kids. His were much younger than me. Back home, at the *Opry*, I had taken his kids out front a couple of times to buy popcorn. He said something to the effect that children were what life was about. He asked about Daddy and Mom and joked that he had seen them more than I had in recent months. He started humming. He got out his fiddle. His feet began to shuffle and next thing I knew, they had introduced him. He went out on that stage, so much like anybody else you'd have a good conversation with, yet so very different.

Mom had sent a "care package" of carob cookies and vitamins by way of Marie. It was just so nice to have a connection to home. After the concert, my friends and I visited on John's tour bus with him and Marie, his manager, their dog, Bus, and so that I could pick up the package. My friends were in awe. I, personally, felt claustrophobic. John was back to his

(l to r) Buck White, John Hartford, and Frazier Moss playing at one of John and Marie's parties in their home in 1983. PHOTOGRAPH BY LES LEVERETT.

old, quiet self. Every bit of energy had been drained from him on the stage. Later, my friends remarked at how silent he was. They couldn't believe that we had, just hours before, had a normal conversation.

John definitely marched to a different drummer. His feet told that story, but his genius underlined it. He was a word master, mixing and matching words to create incredible lyrics and poems. Many of his songs were very humorous, but the one he will be most remembered for is "Gentle on My Mind." Glen Campbell made it a hit in the sixties.

A young boy named Larry Crew in Richmond, Virginia, heard that song on the radio so many times and liked it so much, that he saved his money and purchased the album, the first recording he ever bought. He listened to it repeatedly on the huge console stereo that took up most of his parents' living room. Years later he ended up studying music in college. An audition and job in the music industry brought him to Nashville,

John Hartford's handwritten invitation to his party where Libby met Larry Crew in 1981.

where he ended up living just a few houses down from John Hartford. This is an important story, as you will soon find out the reason.

After spending two summers at the Y, I came home to Nashville. At the time, I really didn't know why. Soon thereafter, my pet dog of thirteen years died. Then my mom had a heart attack. I was definitely needed at home. The real answer to my questions of why I left the most gorgeous place on the U.S. map came later, at a party on the banks of the Cumberland River at John and Marie Hartford's house.

That very day I had told my mother that if I did not meet someone that night at John and Marie's, I was going to join a nunnery or run off with the Peace Corp and never come back. The thought of going back to Colorado again was coming to me more often than not. All my childhood friends had left Nashville. The only constant was my family and the circle of friends I had from the *Opry*.

The occasion was the first anniversary of John and Marie's wedding. It would become an annual event, occurring during the week after Christmas. They had a huge tent set up in their side yard with kerosene heaters and lighting all around. In the warmth of their home were the food, the wassail, and the fireplace. The party went on for three days with people stopping in when they could and staying as long as possible.

That night, Leon Russell, Shel Silverstein, Buck White, Grandpa and Ramona Jones, and John Hartford were playing under the tent. In the house, others were playing in front of the fireplace. There were so many people there and the noise level was so high that I had to take a break. Living in the quiet of the mountains had done something to me, I guess. I sat on a rock wall overlooking the river and let my mind wander. Being with the people I had grown up with was wonderful, but I had broadened

Larry Crew practicing in his home down the river from John Hartfords in 1982. PHOTOGRAPH BY LIBBY LEVERETT-CREW.

Larry and Libby in their garden. PHOTOGRAPH BY LES LEVERETT.

my horizons and really missed living in the Rockies. I was lonely. One of John's many dogs came for a scratch behind the ears. People were coming and going through the door and back to the tent behind me. I heard the familiar sound of Daddy's shutter. Sure enough, he had snuck up on me, as always knowing a special moment when he saw one.

Later, I walked back into the tent and right into one of the most handsome men I had ever seen. His name was Larry. He was a musician and lived a few houses down the street. He told me how he hated camera flashes, then asked what I did. I told him I was a photographer. He blushed. He wondered if I was the photographer's date. No, I let him know that if he looked closely, our profiles were the very same. He was not my date, but my daddy. After he removed his foot from his mouth, he asked if I'd like to go out with him sometime.

On the night of our first date, he stopped by the ATM machine, only to find that it was out of order. Daddy was at the *Opry* that night and Mom was at home. When he came to get me, she was at the dining table tying seventy-five one dollar bills to a money tree for my Grandmother's birthday the next day. As my mother is so good at, she engaged him in conversation while she was handling all that money.

Les Leverett and John Hartford at the reopening of the Ryman
Auditorium in 1994. PHOTOGRAPH BY LIBBY LEVERETT-CREW.

(He later told me he wanted so badly to ask for a loan.) They talked and
talked, and Mom forgot to come and get me. As he helped me into the
car, he asked if I had any money on me. I almost got out right then and
packed my bags to go back to Colorado.

That was over twenty years ago, and I'm glad I didn't. The next time
I went off to Colorado it was about three years later, and I took Larry
with me. It was our honeymoon.

Every year I thanked John and Marie for inviting us to their home during the holidays. They always thought it was cool that a strong romance
had been born at their place. Over the years, Larry and the Hartfords joked
that they shared "grandcats" since the Hartford's tomcat had fathered kit-
tens with Larry and his roommate's female cat. We felt like in-laws.

It always fascinated me that John Hartford and my daddy were such
close friends. John was at times so introverted and odd. Daddy was so
upfront. John was very open-minded about religion, and Daddy was a

The song John wrote for and gave to Les. FROM THE COLLECTION OF LES LEVERETT.

devoted follower of Christ. Yet Daddy had a way of understanding that deep, sometimes dark, minds turned out beautiful works of art. They lived near each other, and Daddy would go over to hang out with John. He had a secret workshop on the lowest floor of their interesting home. The entrance was through a trap door in the den. I can just imagine those two down there, like little boys in a hideout.

They had so many of the same interests, and I guess that's what brought them together. They loved good stories, history, genealogy, well-written books, poetry, the river, good music, and good people. John even wrote a song about Daddy's father called "Walter Be a Good Boy" and gave it to him, all done up in his lovely calligraphy. He had listened as Daddy told him about his father and had stored it away until a fiddle tune came to him. What a mind, a gentle mind.

Les Leverett in front of the *General Jackson* Showboat the night they left for New Orleans in 1990. PHOTOGRAPH BY LIBBY LEVERETT-CREW.

Daddy had gone with John and some other people to carry the *General Jackson* Showboat to winter dry-dock in New Orleans. They stayed up late at night in the pilothouse talking and watching the Mississippi River and then raided the kitchen for coffee, cheese, and peanut butter before retiring to bed. Once they reached New Orleans, Daddy and John explored "The Crescent City" together. My brother Gary flew down to New Orleans on assignment with The Nashville Network film crew to document the *General Jackson's* return trip. John was his roommate. I can just imagine John with his interesting perspective, comparing the similar personality traits between father and son.

For over twenty years John had been dealing with non-Hodgkins lymphoma. His dedication to music fueled his determination to continue performing in spite of his failing health. One of his final appearances was the taping at the Ryman of "Down from the Mountain,"

John Hartford playing with "Red" Rector at Grandpa Jones' home. Alisa Jones is in the background. PHOTOGRAPH BY LES LEVERETT.

featuring the performers from the *O, Brother, Where Art Thou?* soundtrack. John eventually became too sick to play, and that was heartbreaking to him and to those who loved him. He lay on the couch unable to move his once nimble fingers, unable to speak above a whisper. I could not bring myself to go see him, and neither could Gary. Daddy and Mom put it off until it was almost too late. Daddy said he wanted to remember him playing, happy, and healthy. He put aside his own feelings and remembered, upon some encouragement from Mom, that they needed to go, not for themselves, but for John. He needed to know that they cared. They both needed to say goodbye. Daddy could barely talk about their visit until years after John died.

Daddy told me that Norman Blake and his wife Nancy were there, playing tunes for John. If John believed in angels, they were not playing harps, but fiddle tunes. I'm sure of it. With as many friends as he had, a multitude of heavenly hosts played for him. There was a constant stream of people coming by to play for him at the end. They would stop playing and he found a way to whisper for more. Before my parents left, he whispered to them that he loved them.

When John passed away, the world was silent and sadness seemed to settle upon the river. Visitation was at their home where he was lying in state in the living room. Framed in the window behind the wooden casket was John's beloved Cumberland River. It flowed, moving on and on, not stopping even for this.

Outside his home, on the banks of the river, the Coast Guard had built the John Hartford Light, which riverboat pilots use for navigation. It is there forevermore.

The funeral was held in the side yard where for years the same people had gathered on John and Marie's anniversaries to celebrate life. This time, generations of kids and grandkids were there. There was an open mike and the likes of Sam Bush and Earl Scruggs played and sang John into the next world. The *General Jackson*, which John had actually piloted, stopped as it passed by the house and gave a sad blow of its whistle, leaving in its wake waves of sadness and tears of loss. The people on the boat all came to the side and waved in a sympathetic show of support.

The service consisted not only of music, but of people taking turns going up and telling their little stories and memories of their times with John. I knew that Daddy had so much to say and could not, would not. He was so very sad over the loss of his dear friend. I also knew that I had something to share, but I could not stop crying long enough to say two words, much less any two words that would make sense. Many people braved the emotion and told stories of humor and depth. Sam Bush played John's fiddle. Someone else played his banjo.

In all the emotional outpouring, in all the sadness and weeping, I felt a feeling of togetherness. Shel Silverstein had passed on a couple years before. His funeral had been held in the same spot as John's. At John's funeral, I met Shel's son for the first time and his grandchild, so fresh and new to this world. Life was going on. John had brought us together once again for a pickin' and for sharing stories and memories. My daughter and the other children present would carry these with them.

I thought of how every bit of energy we put out remains and comes back around to us again and again. John gave us songs, paintings, and words. He gave us humor and made us all look twice at the river and lis-

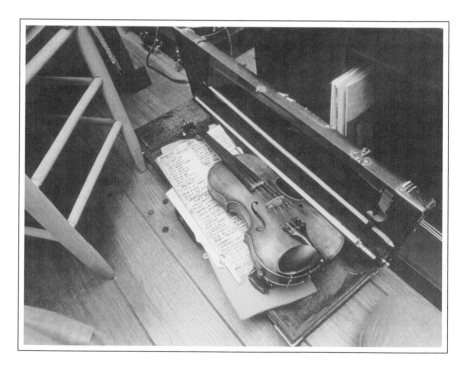

John's fiddle. PHOTOGRAPH BY LES LEVERETT.

ten more to the birds and each other. He brought me together with my soul mate. How could I really be sad?

I think of John very often. When I am near the river, when I see or hear a boat upon the water or hear one of his tunes, it all flows together and comes back around. And John does not seem so far away.

THE FLIGHT OF
THE SONGBIRD

Steam billows from under the bathroom door. I stand outside and listen. Allison, our daughter, is singing in the shower. She makes up a lot of her songs as she goes. Her heartfelt tunes enter into my own heart and tears roll down my cheeks.

Allison Crew singing with her new inflatable guitar that her daddy brought home for her from a gig in 1997. PHOTOGRAPH BY LES LEVERETT.

Allison Crew in 1997. PHOTOGRAPH BY LIBBY LEVERETT-CREW.

On any given day in our home, you can hear our songbird. She sings with such freedom and elation that she is unaware of anything around her. It's contagious, and no matter what is going on in my grown-up world, I am so drawn into this joyous outpouring of unadulterated happiness that I cannot help but feel happy, too. Usually I end up laughing as I cry.

This child and her spirit keep me grounded. She is my constant reminder not just to be alive, but also to be *in* life. We are in the middle of it together and not a day goes by that I do not thank God for the honor of being on life's journey with Allison. She reminds me that there really are no ordinary days. They are each extraordinary. She reminds me to dream and look forward, to never forget the people, places, and experiences of the past, and to always be in the present. All of these have to merge to make us whole. Behold the wisdom of a child! Some of our more "cosmically attuned" friends say that Allison has an old spirit. We joke that she was in heaven so long waiting on us that she learned all of the angels' secrets. Whatever it is, she has always seemed wise beyond her years. I have no doubt she was sent here to help guide me through my life. My life is a continuation of another story, and I feel honored that Allison will continue mine.

I always had a sense of history, even as a child. I knew that our story had progressed from some other time. Some players had gone on. Some new ones had been added. But no matter, the story continued to be told. Even when I was very small, there was a distant narration going on in my head. I was always recording and storing, always observing the details and remembering. I knew that one day it would be my turn to share—to repeat and pass on our family stories.

When my husband, Larry, and I decided to add our branch to the family tree, we had our whole life planned out. After two years of marriage, we would have a baby. Two years later, we'd have another one. We thought we would keep on until we had about four. We went so far as to plan and take one last big trip—just the two of us—before we became parents.

We were young and nothing turned out the way we planned. It just went the way it was supposed to be, but we didn't understand this until much later.

After our trip to Hawaii, three more years passed until finally, we conceived. The news of our pregnancy spread like wildfire through our network of loving friends and family. My brother Gary even put up a notice on the bulletin board backstage at the Opry House. Everyone knew how badly we wanted a baby and shared in our joy. Congratulatory cards arrived and phone calls came in by the dozen.

We had just begun building a large home. It was going to be spacious enough to hold all of those children we were going to have. Everything was falling into place, just a couple of years off from what we had planned. And we could deal with that.

I have not seen my daddy cry many times in my life. But he cried tears of joy when we told him we were expecting.

And he cried for two days when we found out that our baby was not going to make it into the world. I miscarried at four months. It was the saddest thing that had ever happened to me.

This was my first realization that life absolutely cannot be planned.

Larry and I would go out to check on the construction of our home just to have something to look forward to. I would invariably end up standing in the middle of the unfinished room that was to be the nursery and bawl my eyes out.

For the next several years, everything seemed overshadowed by that loss and the fact that we still did not have a child. When our big, new home was completed, the nursery became my art room. During this time, we went through infertility testing, to no avail (we were labeled "unexplained"), and simultaneously began adoption procedures.

My mother was thirty-three when I was born. The year that *I* turned thirty-three, a young girl came into my life who was expecting a child she loved dearly but could not raise. A mutual friend brought us together, knowing we were looking for a child to adopt. Together we entered into an open adoption.

Libby holding Allison in 1993. PHOTOGRAPH BY LARRY CREW.

My life changed course the day that Allison was placed in my arms. This must have been how my daddy felt that day when he saw the ocean for the first time. I knew that there was so much more out there. There were going to be adventures and sandboxes beyond belief.

Here was this tiny, helpless baby. Her life was so fragile, her slate so clean, and my job, as her parent was to fill that slate with goodness, knowledge, and love. I was to protect her from the evils of the world and introduce her to all of its wonders. It was going to be a great journey.

When we became parents, I began to see Larry in a new light. There is nothing more heartwarming than seeing a strong man holding a small child. He adores Allison. I watch them together and smile. He shares his love of music with her, and just like my relationship with my father, they share many of the same dreams.

I will never forget the look of sheer elation on Daddy's face the day

Larry holding Allison in 1993. This is Libby's favorite photograph of the two of them together to date. PHOTOGRAPH BY LIBBY LEVERETT-CREW.

that our daughter came home with us. We did not tell my parents we were getting our baby, and on that Saturday afternoon, we just showed up on their doorstep with our bundle of joy. Daddy, being the perceptive photographer that he is, grabbed his camera and caught Mom's reaction as she opened the door. Our placement day was a major tearfest. We passed Allison around and marveled at how perfect she was.

Today, if I curl my arms up in front of my chest, I can still feel her there, our hearts beating next to each other, her warmth reaching into my very soul.

That day, holding her in our arms, we realized that no matter what you plan that does not work out, no matter how much you believe that things will not work out, everything actually does. When things fall into place, it is so perfect, so very magical, that you wonder why you ever worried, why you ever wasted time trying so hard to plan and make things happen.

There we were, after all of those years of trying and waiting, holding the most precious gift we were ever to receive. She was finally here to begin her journey with us. She, and the way she came to us, is the greatest example of hope that I can think of.

Now, when I hear my songbird in the shower, I am forced to stop what I am doing and listen to what's really important in my life.

Her musical abilities seem to be an inborn talent. Yet, the influence of her father's gift and career has also no doubt had an impact. If I had not had Saturday nights with my daddy at the *Opry*, I may have taken a different path in my life. If my mother had not gone to work with her

Les (P-Pa, or Peeps) with Allison in 1993. PHOTOGRAPH BY LIBBY LEVERETT-CREW.

Allison learning how to play bass with "Dahdee" in 1994. PHOTOGRAPH BY LIBBY LEVERETT-CREW.

daddy and witnessed his kindness toward others, she would not have been the thoughtful, wonderful person that she became. Having a father who shows interest in his daughter, who spends genuine, quality time exploring life with his girl is a priceless treasure.

Allison has songs that just come to her, maybe from some universal pool of knowledge, or maybe from the angels above, who knows? It is amazing to see how easily she can write a tune with lyrics. This is her gift, and along with her voice, I'm sure she will follow in her daddy's footsteps straight into a musical career. Music is her love, her passion. Our job as her parents is to help nurture this in her.

Just as in my childhood, there is an eclectic collection of music in our home. We go from classical to Motown, from bluegrass to rock 'n' roll, from country to jazz. Allison has been exposed to all genres of music.

When Larry is practicing his bass guitar, Allison sometimes sits in his lap and he leads her through some notes and lets her play. He has done this with her since she was a baby. She likes the way you can feel the electricity in the strings and the way the bass sounds so strong and bold. Sometimes the two of them jam on her violin and his flute, and recently, she wrote a song in which they worked out the melody together.

Allison's first trip into the recording studio was when she was two months old. She often goes with her daddy to live gigs and recording sessions. He lets her carry some of his equipment. She takes in the way he works with people, his kind, gentle character, and the energy that you can only find in an orchestra pit or on a stage in front of hundreds of people. She watches the dancers, listens to the singers, observes the way a recording comes together, and, no doubt, dreams.

Allison's first trip into the recording studio "to work" with her daddy in 1993. They are sitting at the piano on which Carole King recorded the *Tapestry* album. PHOTOGRAPH BY LIBBY LEVERETT-CREW.

Allison teething on my lens cap and playing with a film canister during her P-Pa's induction into the Star Walk in Nashville in 1994. PHOTOGRAPH BY LIBBY LEVERETT-CREW.

I did not know the depth of my parents' love for me, nor could I fully understand our connection until I became a parent myself. I had waited a very long time for a child to come into my life, and now that she's here, I treasure every little thing about her.

Actually, I have turned into emotional mush since I became Allison's mother. I cry at the oddest times. She was so tiny, so helpless, and now she is already at the midpoint of her childhood. Who knew the time would go by so fast? (Now I know why my parents look at my graying hair in disbelief). The baby that I once held in my arms, now comes up to my shoulder. I can no longer scoop her up into my lap or swing her by the hands in the tall grass. She stands alone. She is her own person, a confident girl with a voice of her own. I watch in awe as she finds her way in this world.

While life is zooming by, we are in the middle of it, enjoying every moment we have together. And she always reminds me that this is what's important. This is what life is all about. So many things have changed since my Saturday nights at the *Opry* with Daddy. Many people have played their roles and moved on.

One cool, early spring morning I had to tell my parents that their firstborn, my oldest brother, had been killed in an automobile accident. It was the hardest thing I have ever had to do. Daddy came to the door of my childhood home, glad, as always to see me, yet knowing that something was terribly wrong. I made him sit down. I wrapped my arms around his neck and whispered the news. All of a sudden, I was playing the role of

Allison jamming with her dad in 1999. PHOTOGRAPH BY LIBBY LEVERETT-CREW.

Allison in 1997 singing and playing on the same old piano that Marty Robbins played and Dolly Parton sang with. PHOTOGRAPH BY LIBBY LEVERETT-CREW.

an adult. For obvious reasons, I had always felt like the child of the household. I was always "the baby." Daddy had never seemed old to me. In my eyes, he and my mother had never aged. As Daddy took my hand and led me to their bedroom to wake Mom, he was shuffling. His back

Allison Crew performing with the strings orchestra at her school in 2002.
PHOTOGRAPH BY LIBBY LEVERETT-CREW.

was bent over. His blue eyes were faded. Surprisingly, he seemed old. I felt old, and I realized that our family dynamics had changed.

As our family and friends gathered to grieve in my childhood home, Allison disappeared. We found her under Daddy's desk writing poetry about families.

My family consists of what I was born into, and part of my family is the ever-changing cast of the *Opry*, and all the other people who keep music in our lives. Following in Daddy's footsteps, I went into photography and he and I worked many jobs together in the music and convention industry. There was a running joke at the *Opry* that I had no name of my own. I was "Les's daughter." When my brother began working at the *Opry*, I then became, "Les's daughter and Gary's little sister."

The *Opry* moved to a new location. Joyously, the Ryman Auditorium was refurbished and is in use again. During the winter months, the *Opry* again broadcasts from the Ryman. Daddy and I were commissioned to print and handcolor the photographs that decorate the new backstage areas, dressing rooms, and the display boxes out in front of our beloved Ryman Auditorium. It was an honor to work side-by-side with my daddy, using the skills that I had learned from him. And, I have learned so much by his side.

Libby and Les together at the reopening of the Ryman in 1994 in front of one of the display boxes holding their handcolored photographs. PHOTOGRAPH BY LARRY CREW.

Allison helping her P-Pa check over his new book at the printers in 1996.
PHOTOGRAPH BY LIBBY LEVERETT-CREW.

One of the things I enjoy most about being a parent is watching my child with my daddy. I see him repeating the role he played in my life, but from a different angle.

When we take Allison to my parents' house, we play an inning or two of baseball. We run through the yard and play wonderful games of hide-and-seek. We climb trees, explore the creek and garden, pick flowers, play on the tire swing, and even have treasure hunts. The memories of my childhood days there are so far away, yet so very fresh. My red sandbox is long gone, but I feel its magical presence in that yard. Allison brings my childhood back to me on a daily basis.

After an afternoon in my parents' yard, Allison typically ends up in Daddy's office. They listen to music and discuss each song. I walk by, listen, and peek in. Stacks of negatives, slides, and prints sit around this

Les Leverett showing Allison a bird near the creek in the backyard in 1995. PHOTOGRAPH BY LIBBY LEVERETT-CREW.

office. His Grammy Award sits on a shelf. Dozens of album covers with his
photographs are in racks nearby. Until she got too big to do so, Allison

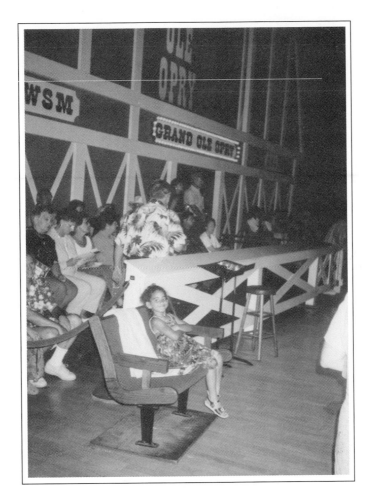

Allison Crew sitting on the *Opry* stage in 1997 during a
performance. PHOTOGRAPH BY LES LEVERETT.

would sit in Daddy's lap at his desk and the two of them would draw while
they listened to the tunes. Now, he sits in command by his stereo, and
Allison has out all of his pens on his desk, drawing what comes to her as
the music plays. He looks over at her with a gleam in his eye.

He knows she will remember these days. She will know a Tex Ritter
song, a Grandpa Jones banjo tune, or a Minnie Pearl joke when she

hears one. She will tell her children about this very moment, this extraordinary day with her grandfather. Our songbird will go home to play her violin and sing with her daddy as he plays his bass. She is sur-rounded by love, laughter, and music. What more does anyone need?

The music will play on, and our story will continue . . .

INDEX

Italics numbers refer to pages with illustrations.